Cripple Creek Bonanza

A John Cunningham
from
Harold "Take" Reynolds

Chet Cunningham

Republic of Texas Press

Library of Congress Cataloging-in-Publication Data

Cunningham, Chet.
    Cripple creek bonanza / Chet Cunningham.
      p.   cm.
    ISBN 1-55622-399-4 (pbk.)
    1. Cripple Creek (Colo.)--History.   2. Cripple Creek (Colo.)--Gold
    discoveries.   3. Gold mines and mining--Colorado--Cripple Creek--
    History.   I. Title.
    F784.C8C87   1995
    987.8'58--dc20   95-20831
                                                                     CIP

Copyright © 1996, Chet Cunningham

Printed in the United States of America

ISBN1-55622-399-4
10 9 8 7 6 5 4 3 2 1
9511

All inquiries for volume purchases of this book should be addressed
to Wordware Publishing, Inc., at 1506 Capital Avenue, Plano, Texas
75074. Telephone inquiries may be made by calling:
                    (214) 423-0090

Contents

Dedication

To Celinda and Harold
Kaelin of Florissant
who helped immensely
with this book. And
to Birdie....
the burro.

CHAPTER 1

The Float Find

From the first discovery of gold at Cripple Creek, Colorado, in 1891 right into the late 1990s, the small village has been on a wild roller coaster ride of ups and downs that is now on the upswing again.

From "Crazy" Bob Womack and his find of a large piece of "float," gold bearing ore broken off a hidden vein of gold years before, to the huge earth moving machines now mining gold from ore with 0.03 of an ounce per ton yield, Cripple Creek has produced a vivid array of colorful characters, millionaires, madams, a war almost fought during a miner's union strike, and now a small, stable village experiencing the blessings and pitfalls of Las Vegas type limited gambling. Big business has moved in on the old mining claims, and one mining company now hopes to take out more than $800 million worth of gold from Cripple Creek's mining district within the next ten years—by strip mining.

How did the saga of Cripple Creek get started? Bob Womack and his brother, William, had homesteaded side-by-side 160-acre plots in the area below Mount Pisgah. It was on a place known as the old Welty Ranch. Welty had

1

squatted there for years and sold his squatter's rights to the Womacks. Then they homesteaded. This area was twenty miles from the Womack home place over the mountains near Little Fountain Creek. There the family cattle business was centered on four plots of land owned by brothers Bob and William and sister Miss Lida and their father.

BOB WOMACK the founder of the Cripple Creek gold rush. A cowboy, a prospector, a drinker, a loner who loved the chase, the looking and finding gold more than he did mining it and getting rich. He led the charge into Cripple Creek and because of him thirty men became millionaires, Colorado Springs tripled in size, and he founded the village of Cripple Creek. Bob died without funds. (Photo Courtesy Colorado Springs Pioneer Museum)

Bob Womack participated in the family business, became adept at riding and roping, and often drove part of the herd of cattle from the Sunview Ranch on Little Fountain Creek to better grazing on his and his brother's homesteads below Mount Pisgah.

Bob was on one of these cattle drives when he paused at a small stream that ran near the old Welty spring house to let the animals drink.

For years Bob had been prospecting whenever he had a chance and had scoured the lands around Mount Pisgah with no luck. He had found what was known as "float," but usually they were small pieces of gold ore that might have come from anywhere.

This day, May 7, 1878, he spotted an interesting rock near the water and retrieved it, a chunk of gray stone about nine inches long.

He later told friends he knew at once it was a piece of float, the largest he had ever found. Float such as this would have been a part of an outcropping of quartz or other gold bearing ore. Then, due to erosion or freezing or for some other reason, the rock had broken off the outcropping and "floated," rolled, or been washed down from somewhere on the slopes above. The small valley where Bob found the float is nearly barren of vegetation now and must have looked about the same then in this semiarid land. It is rocky, with a few wild raspberry bushes, weeds, and a little low brush.

That day Bob Womack discovered the piece of float which eventually would lead to the Cripple Creek Bonanza, but that event wouldn't happen for another thirteen years.

During the spring of 1878, Bob Womack turned thirty-four years old. He was a bachelor, stood six feet tall, strong as a brown bear, and had black hair that had lost a fight with a receding hairline. His ears, larger than normal, fit well with his prominent nose and flaring nostrils. He looked at the world from dark, deep-set eyes.

Bob must have hefted the rock. All prospectors knew that float was lighter in color and weight than a comparable chunk of normal rock. This rock fit the description. Bob Womack probably looked up the gully of the small creek and figured that the float must have come from somewhere up this mile-long ravine. But where? He had searched this area dozens of times and had never found an upthrust of any kind.

As the prospectors of that day knew, the upthrust from where this piece of float came could have been covered over hundreds of years ago by wind-whipped dirt or a landslide. By now the upthrust he searched for could be fifty feet underground.

The other possibility was that the gold bearing ore could have been loosened a thousand years ago, and the spot it came from could now be mashed down and eroded away or ground into gold dust by some massive earth movement. Such gold dust could now be a hundred miles downstream on some river. Then there would be no mother lode.

Two weeks later Bob Womack took time off from his herding and cowboy chores and rode his horse Whistler twenty-five miles to Colorado Springs, where the millionaire General William Jackson Palmer had established his "cultural oasis in a desert of American savagery" in 1871. People called the place Little London because it pretended to be more British than London and more or less succeeded.

Colorado Springs had been established by General Palmer as a resort in the best European style. It was a plush haven for the rich, a hideaway for invalids from wealthy families, a center for retired capitalists. It catered to spoiled continentals who couldn't stand Switzerland anymore and a getaway where the elite of Eastern American society could take advantage of the climate, the altitude, and the fine hunting and fishing.

Colorado Springs quickly grew to ten thousand people and had all the luxuries and comforts that wealth and the railroad could bring them in the year of 1878.

At the Springs, Bob mailed his chunk of float to a long-time family friend, Theodore Lowe, who lived in Denver. He asked Lowe to have the float sample assayed.

Three days later, Lowe hurried to Bob's shack on his homestead to tell him the news.

Lowe told him that at first the assayer said the sample wasn't worth spending thirty-five cents to get assayed. He called it a piece of rotten old rock. Lowe had insisted, and the results showed that the float assayed out as gold bearing ore worth $200 a ton. Now all the two men had to do was find the mother lode and get rich.

For more than a week both of them scoured the hillside above the Welty Ranch well house where the small creek came down. They inched up the valley, looking for any indication that the ground cover might be masking an upthrust of gold bearing quartz. They worked every small gully and ravine that joined the main one. It turned out to be a tedious and backbreaking job.

After a week, Lowe told Bob he had to get back to work. He had a family to feed. He urged Bob to keep looking. They both knew that the float meant there had to be an upthrust with ore in it worth $200 a ton somewhere up that small creek watershed.

He kept at it, searching for the spot where a crack in the bedrock had let hot liquid rock veined with gold shoot to the surface before it cooled. That would be his bonanza.

He kept working now and again herding cattle, putting in time at the ranch. When he wasn't driving cattle he kept searching for the upthrust.

Bob was described by friends as an indifferent cowboy, losing as many cattle as he saved. He often vanished for days at a time, prospecting or sampling the whiskey and gambling over at Colorado City, a small town three miles from the Springs where gambling was legal.

The stream below the Welty cabin had earned a name. The few cattlemen in the area called it Cripple Creek. It came about one day when a cow, a horse, and a cowboy all fell into the stream and broke bones. The cowboy called it a blasted cripple creek. The name stuck.

Whenever he had time, Bob Womack prospected the area above the spring house that he had named Poverty Gulch. The float had to have come from up there somewhere.

Often when Bob found a likely spot, he dug a shaft straight down ten or twelve feet searching for the top of the upthrust that had produced the $200-a-ton chunk of float. He didn't find the upthrust.

Years slipped by. Bob kept working on the main ranch and digging more holes, looking for his upthrust. He and his brother William had preemption patents on land at Sunview Ranch and their homesteads near Mount Pisgah to keep in force. Bob wasn't fond of ranching, but he did like to ride and became an expert. He could do several tricks from horseback and loved showing off.

For the next three years, Bob dug shafts, prospected, and worked at the ranch. All the time he kept trying to find his bonanza.

Now and then Bob spent a few days at Colorado City, playing faro or poker and gulping down bad whiskey. He went to Colorado City because General Palmer allowed no sale of whiskey or gambling in his town three miles away.

Bob bragged a bit about his bonanza, about the float worth $200 a ton. Soon the stories about his "bonanza" were known in every saloon in Colorado City. The more Bob drank, the wilder his claims became. But through it all he stuck to his point, he had found float assayed at $200 a ton. Nobody else had done that. Soon few in the saloons believed anything Bob Womack had to say about his gold find.

One slight, bearded newcomer to town, a Cornishman named Henry Cocking, listened to Bob's story with puzzlement. He said he'd never heard a drunk keep his story so straight and be so vehement defending it. The Cornishman came from England and had been a hard rock miner all his life. He talked to Bob about the float.

It was 1881 by then and Bob had worked up the float trail almost a mile to a point east of the Welty cabin and on the west side of Poverty Gulch.

Cocking showed up at Bob's place one day and looked over the scene. He found a number of small pieces of float scattered about. After a search of the area, he staked a claim at the highest point to where Bob had followed his float trail. Cocking dug a shaft and then a tunnel into hard rock that at that site was stained with iron pyrites. He found no new float and no gold.

Years later it was discovered that Cocking had stopped his tunnel only three feet short of breaking into a vein that produced over three million dollars in gold. If Cocking had dug another three feet, the Cripple Creek gold rush would have erupted ten years earlier than it did.

Henry Cocking went back to Denver, but Bob Womack kept trying to find his upthrust.

Three years later, in 1884, Bob's brother William tired of the cattle business. He and his wife wanted to go back to Kentucky. In the summer of that year, Bob and William sold their homesteads and cattle, and William and his family returned to Kentucky.

The new owners of the cattle ranch knew little of the business and soon sold the place to two businessmen from Denver. They let Bob keep his shack on Poverty Gulch near the edge of the ranch.

The new owners, Horace Bennett and Julius Myers, promptly hired veteran cattleman George Carr, who knew how to make a ranch pay. He moved in and put the cattle operation on a firm footing.

Bob kept to his shack, worked part-time for Carr on the ranch, and continued digging holes looking for his big strike. He kept drinking and gambling in Colorado City and soon became the butt of jokes and a laughing stock there and in Colorado Springs. He was teased about his wild "bonanza" tales and was soon dubbed "Crazy" Bob Womack.

The slumbering gold field was not impressed and lay where it had been for a million years. Not more than a dozen ranchers lived near Mount Pisgah. There was no town of Cripple Creek.

Through it all, Bob kept digging, searching, and sweating to find his upthrust. It was seven long years more before Crazy Bob Womack at last found his upthrust. It erupted into the richest gold rush in the Colorado Rockies.

CHAPTER 2

The Grannis Partnership

In December of 1889 Bob Womack went to a dentist in Colorado Springs to have a tooth filled. A few months before, the dentist had bought into Bob's marginal placer claims up on the plains near the Womack's Sunview Ranch on Little Fountain Creek. Everyone involved lost money on the worthless claims.

The dentist, Dr. John P. Grannis, had come west to recover from tuberculosis. He set up a practice in the Springs. Far from wealthy, Dr. Grannis suffered substantial losses on the placers, and this concerned Bob.

Dr. Grannis, a tall, slender man still with vestiges of his cough and a pale complexion, had a burning desire to whip his T.B. and make a name for himself in his new hometown. He had a long face, with deep-set eyes, thin brows, and a receding blond hairline. The Springs residents were not easily impressed, and he made little progress in gaining a toehold in the upper crust of the local society.

While with the dentist, Bob talked on and on about his gold finding ability and his $200-a-ton piece of float and his prospecting. The dentist, though a newcomer to the Springs, had learned quickly about the Mount Pisgah salted mine hoax and all the stories that had circulated about "Crazy" Bob Womack during the past eleven years. Nevertheless, he showed interest in Womack's burning conviction that there had to be gold in Poverty Gulch.

Dr. Grannis invited Bob to his home so they could talk more. The dentist became fascinated with gold prospecting and bought books and consulted the local experts.

He learned that Poverty Gulch could be part of the site of an ancient volcano that erupted and blew the top off a massive mountain. Bob's chunk of float might have come from a volcanic chimney or a crack through which the mineral rich volcanic core had spewed up the gold and other precious metals, and they solidified in the cracks somewhere close to the surface of the barren and rocky confines of Poverty Gulch.

Dr. Grannis talked to Bob Womack again on December 2, 1889 and presented him with a check for $500.

It was a grubstake. Now Bob would have enough money for tools and equipment and food so he could concentrate on digging up the bonanza in Poverty Gulch. They were fifty-fifty partners in whatever he developed.

His first expenditure with his grubstake money was six bottles of beer, and that led to a two-day drunk. The third day he spent twelve dollars on a pair of blue pants and a new pair of boots and promptly left Colorado Springs for his diggings in Poverty Gulch.

Bob Womack must have felt like a new man. Somebody believed in him. No longer must he ride over to Sunview Ranch on Fountain Creek to borrow a few dollars from his sister, Miss Lida. Now he worked with a new fervor.

Winter arrived in the high country. Poverty Gulch is at the 9,600-foot level, but that year's winter was not severe. Bob prospected every day that the elements permitted. With the arrival of the new green leaves of spring of 1890, he renewed his efforts, concentrating for a time around the Grand View claim he had staked in '88 and later abandoned. He worked over the whole Poverty Gulch area again that summer and then went back to the Grand View site.

Toward the east side of his first claim, he discovered more and more small pieces of float much like the original gray one he had found. This in itself seemed unusual. A dozen pieces of float from the same upthrust, once deposited on the surface, can take on all sorts of different colors and hues and weights depending on where each piece of gold bearing rock has been lying and what elements of the weather attacked it.

He kept finding more small pieces of the float until he knew he had to do some digging. Bob picked out the most logical spot to hold an upthrust and began to move dirt.

He drove a four-foot-wide shaft into the soft earth and rocks with his pick and shovel to a depth of ten feet, hauling the dirt out with a bucket on a rope and a windlass.

When the shaft was finished, he dug a short drift from the bottom of the hole eastward. The work intensified. He had to put two kerosene lanterns in the three-foot-high drift so he had light to work by. Then he loaded the dirt and rocks in buckets and hauled them back to the shaft where he lifted them to the surface and dumped them out.

When three eastern angled tunnels twenty feet long were unproductive, he dug two more drifts, this time northeast. Then he angled one due north. On the north tunnel after thirty feet, he found more and more of the small pieces of float.

By the middle of October 1890, he still worked the north tunnel hoping that the float would stop and he'd find an upthrust. Now the task grew harder. He had farther to drag out the earth and rocks. To make the tunneling go faster, he cut the top of the north drift down to two and a half feet, until he barely had room to crawl through pulling the buckets of dirt and rocks.

Once at the central shaft, he still had to climb his ladder to the surface and pull up the buckets and dump them out. Then he decided to empty the buckets of dirt and rocks in the unproductive drifts, saving the long trip. It still remained tedious, slow, backbreaking work.

The date was October 20, 1890, when Bob Womack climbed down the ladder into the shaft and then along the north tunnel for another day of digging. On his first shovel of dirt that morning, he struck something hard. He pounded the front of the tunnel with the spade again and felt the same result.

Quickly he dug away the dirt and rocks and found a solid upthrust of dense rock that looked nearly round and two feet in diameter. He dug upward along the rock shaft until he found the top. Four feet above the bottom of the tunnel he came to the peak of the column of hard rock. He brushed it off, scattering the dirt of centuries. He reached down and lifted the lantern and sat it on the rock column. Then he could see that the middle of the pillar showed a deep discoloration. Right in the center of that dark area lay a half-inch-wide crack filled with gold ore. That crack represented his gold mine. He had struck it rich at last.

He dug upward then, pushing the dirt and rocks behind him in his tunnel. He worked hard and soon broke through to the surface ten feet above the floor of his north tunnel. He had been at it all morning.

Bob checked the midday sun and decided he had time enough for a dynamite blast. He hurried to his shack for three sticks of dynamite, a detonator cap, fuse, and an eight-pound sledge. He also took back a spoon with a three-foot handle, a single jack, a three-foot rock drill, and a bottle full of water.

Bob studied the outcropping. He placed his rock drill three inches from the center of the crack and began to strike the drill head with the eight-pound hammer. After each blow, he made a quarter turn with the drill. Slowly the bit dug into the hard rock. He poured water into the hole to wet the powered rock produced by the drilling.

Regularly he scooped the wet, gray rock powder from the hole with the long-handled spoon, then went on drilling.

When he had the hole thirty inches into the upthrust, he put his tools aside and inserted the waterproof fuse into the hollow end of a primer cap and pushed the cap into a hole he poked in one of the sticks of dynamite. He put the dynamite with the fuse at the bottom of the thirty-inch-deep hole in the hard rock upthrust with the fuse extending upward out of the hole.

Directly over the first dynamite stick he lowered another one down the hole, and then a third. The first dynamite stick would be set off by the fuse and detonator, and a sympathetic explosion would detonate the other two. The three eight-inch dynamite sticks extended twenty-four inches up from the bottom of the hole.

Next he unrolled his five-foot-long length of fuse. It would burn a foot a minute if all went correctly. He poured dirt and small rocks into the bored hole on top of the dynamite until the hole filled. Then he tamped the dirt down firmly.

Bob checked everything again and took all of his tools out of the hole. Then he went back to the fuse, stretched it out flat, and lit it with a match. He climbed out of the hole and walked fifty yards away and knelt behind a hump of earth. He'd found his bonanza!

Five minutes after Bob lit the fuse, an explosion shook Poverty Gulch. When the dirt and rocks stopped falling, Bob ran up to the shaft. He could see little. The sides of the hole had caved in and the outcropping itself must have shattered and broken up in the dirt and rubble.

It would take him all day to dig out the dirt and find all of the gold ore. He dropped into the shaft and pawed at the dirt. Under a foot of the rubble, he found the shattered up-thrust. The crack in the center of the rock had split and he found several chunks that showed the heavy ore. Gold!

He'd clean out the rocks and dirt and separate the gold ore from it, but that was for tomorrow.

Bob walked to his cabin for a pint of whiskey and then on past the old Welty spring house to the Carr's cabin. He told them about his strike he had named the El Paso. He showed them some of the gold ore. Then he poured the amber drinks for George and Emma Carr and the hired man Jack Edwards. They all hoisted their glasses toasting the success of the El Paso claim.

Then Bob Womack went back to his shack and to bed. He would be up with the sun the next morning to get to work on his bonanza.

The next morning, Bob had signs to post on his claim. He measured a 300-by-1,500-foot rectangle on the north side of the gulch using a twenty-foot length of rope. He had laid out the standard size Colorado hard rock mine claim.

Then he pounded in his corner stakes and put up his new notice sign. It read:

El Paso Claim. Located Oct. 20, 1890, by R. M. Womack and Dr. John Grannis. Mining district unknown.

Two days after the strike, "Crazy" Bob Womack rode to Colorado Springs and hurried into the dental office. He barged into the first room where Dr. Grannis worked filling a tooth and showed him the ore he'd found.

The next day, Dr. Grannis and Bob hired Professor Henry Lamb from Colorado College in the Springs to ride out with them and to evaluate the strike. The professor chipped off some ore samples from the upthrust and the next day tested them in his laboratory at the college. The samples assayed out at $250 a ton.

Late that night in the dental office, Dr. Grannis and Bob Womack talked over the future of the El Paso strike.

The next step was to dig out the ore. When they had enough, they would haul it by wagon to the Colorado Midland railroad at Florissant and then ship it to a mill where it would be processed and the gold extracted from the ore. Only then would they get paid for the gold in the ore.

They would need more cash. Bob didn't have any. He knew that Dr. Grannis wasn't rich. But to do the job right they needed manpower, wagons, lift machinery, and timbers for shoring up the tunnels and dozens of other supplies. They would need about fifteen thousand dollars.

If they could get fifteen people to loan them a thousand each at seven percent interest, they would have it.

A week later, Bob Womack and Dr. Grannis gave up. Nobody would even talk to them about a loan. They had been laughed out of one office after another.

Dr. Grannis talked to Hiram Rogers at the *Colorado Springs Gazette*, asking him to look at the ore from the upthrust. Rogers checked it and shrugged. He said he'd seen a hundred chunks of ore like this. If he did a story about every one, he'd have a paper full of them. He assured the dentist that when they shipped out the first wagon of gold ore from the El Paso, he would write up the story.

Bob went on a week-long binge.

Dr. Grannis left a display of Bob's gold ore in the window of the Seldomridge Grain Company, hoping someone might see it there and get interested in financing the mine. Then he went back to filling teeth.

When Bob Womack returned to his El Paso strike, he hacked away at the upthrust. The vein of gold was small. It had to lead to a much thicker, richer vein below, but he didn't have the men or the money to get to it.

If the vein had been six inches wide at the surface, he could have blasted and dug out the ore himself, hired a wagon, hauled the ore to the railroad, and sold it for enough money to hire a few men and dig out more ore and then hire more men. He'd found his strike, but for want of $15,000 to develop it, the upthrust and its vein of gold might as well have been a thousand feet underground and undiscovered.

CHAPTER 3

Ed De La Vergne Checks Out Cripple Creek

Ed De La Vergne was the son of wealthy parents, and he followed them to Colorado Springs when his father retired there. Ed had been bitten by the mining bug early and had wandered from the Ruby silver district north of Gunnison, Colorado, to the Old Man mine at Camp Fleming and then the Blackhawk mine in New Mexico. Nothing proved out.

He tried the Orient silver mines at Lawson, Colorado, but never found the vein or the situation he wanted. After each scramble into mining failed, Ed returned to the family home in Colorado Springs to recoup his finances and his determination.

Ed took Professor Henry Lamb's assaying course at Colorado College there in the Springs and in December of 1890 noticed the display of Bob Womack's gold ore in the Seldomridge Grain Company window.

He talked to Henry Seldomridge about it and had the merchant arrange a meeting the next day with Dr. Grannis, Bob Womack, and Professor Lamb. Ed would be there with a friend, Fred Frisbee.

Professor Lamb explained the theory that the whole Cripple Creek area probably was the cauldron of a giant volcano that blew its top thousands of years ago. The crater had been partially filled in over the centuries and could hold precious metals vomited up from the bowels of the earth.

Ed sat and listened closely but said little. Bob had talked about one or two upthrusts that had gold in them. Ed knew that small pieces of float containing gold had been found in many areas of the Cripple Creek cauldron. Why wouldn't there be upthrusts all over the 10,000 acres of the old cauldron surrounding Cripple Creek?

When the meeting was over Ed did not offer to bankroll the El Paso claim but went away with a desire to explore the Cripple Creek area for himself.

He talked Fred Frisbee into working with him on the prospecting venture and took him and two men and headed for Cripple Creek at the end of January.

They became lost in a snowstorm, almost froze to death, and wandered into the Carr cabin where they thawed out and recovered on Emma Carr's hot coffee and good food.

The next morning they borrowed horses from George Carr and began exploring the area. They spent a month checking out the entire cauldron, pointing out the old rim and finding bits of gold bearing float. They picked out possible sites for staking claims.

Before they went back to Colorado Springs late in February, Ed had staked two claims. The El Dorado was right next to Bob Womack's El Paso claim. He also staked the Old Mortality to the west of the El Dorado.

In the meantime, Bob Womack had tired of trying to find financing for his mine from people in Colorado Springs. He talked Dr. Grannis into another $600 grubstake, bought new supplies, and took them to Florissant by the Colorado Midland railroad.

He tarried there a few days and quickly learned that several more claims had been filed in Cripple Creek. The Blanche, the Hobo, and the Blue Bell had been staked. One man could stake as many claims as he wanted to under Colorado mining laws.

In Florissant the talk was of gold fever. The men in Cripple Creek had gotten together and decided to hold a miner's meeting at the Carr cabin on April 5 with the purpose of setting up a mining district according to Colorado mining law. Nobody was making fun of Bob's find now.

On April 5, 1891 a dozen prospectors gathered at the Carr ranch house to organize. They talked about the size of the district and determined that it should be larger than the apparent boundaries of the cauldron from the old volcano. They called it the Cripple Creek Mining District and set the boundaries as Rhyolite Mountain to the north, Big Bull Hill to the east, Straug Mountain to the south, and Mount Pisgah on the west. That was an area about six miles by six miles, over 23,000 acres.

They set up limits on placer claims. One man could claim twenty acres. All he had to do was stake it and notify the county clerk in Colorado Springs. For his placer claim, the owner had rights to the sand, soil, and gravel down to bedrock, but no deeper.

Any number of persons could go together on adjoining placer claims and get rights to a large block of land: six claims = 120 acres. The ranchers on the committee didn't think placer mining would be a factor, but the placer claims could be used for other purposes, including laying out a townsite.

Ed De La Vergne asked if Bob Womack's claim was to be declared the first strike in the district. Emma Carr and a dozen other miners agreed that he certainly was the man who found the first gold strike.

After some discussion, Bob Womack's El Paso claim was declared the "Discovery Shaft," and he would be known as the man who first found gold and opened the Cripple Creek gold rush.

They elected George Carr president of the mining district.

Bob Womack attended the prospector's meeting, but he huddled in a corner and didn't say a word. He watched the proceedings aware that now there were men running all over Cripple Creek. He nipped on a bottle of bourbon now and again.

Near the end of the meeting, George Carr gave a eulogy of Bob Womack as the man whose faith and courage had brought them all this great opportunity. Loud applause and cheers rose from the miners. Bob nodded in recognition, then bent his head and lowered his eyes. At the urging of the men, Bob grinned broadly at them, sat up straight, and waved. Then he passed out.

Word had leaked out about the El Paso, and the news was that the Cripple Creek area was the new Colorado gold bonanza. The story spread.

That spring and summer a flood of tenderfeet and old pro prospectors descended on Cripple Creek. Claim stakes went up fast.

One morning in early May, Bob Womack heard someone pounding on the door of his shack. He scrabbled out and opened it to find a friend from Colorado Springs, Winfield Scott Stratton. He was a carpenter from the Springs who had been bitten by the mining bug for years. He'd been grubstaked with $275 to go find gold by a friend in the

Springs. Now he was tired and discouraged and told Bob that Cripple Creek was the worst prospecting spot he'd ever seen.

Bob Womack brought out a pint of whiskey for him and Stratton to share for breakfast and they talked. Bob couldn't stand anyone badmouthing Cripple Creek's potential. After the unusual breakfast, Bob gave Stratton a guided tour. Stratton rode his scabby donkey, and Bob was on Whistler.

Bob took him on a tour of Poverty Gulch and Gold Hill, pointing out all of the newly staked claims and the work being done. Bob helped Stratton stake a claim on Gold Hill called the Lone Star.

Stratton complained about all of the tenderfeet who had flocked into the camp. Most of them knew nothing about mining, nothing about how to stake a claim or put up a tent.

Stratton and his partner moved down to the Wilson Creek area near the southern boundary of the district and put up their tent on the far side of Battle Mountain. No tenderfeet there.

He staked some claims and abandoned them and the first week in June headed for Colorado Springs. He would be back. Somehow he couldn't forget what he had seen on Battle Mountain and a ledge that ran along one slope. He'd tested it when he was there and it contained no gold. Still he had a strange feeling about the ledge of granite.

Bob Womack sat back and watched the community grow. In May 1891 a hundred tenderfeet swept into Cripple Creek. In June there were two hundred, and in July a full four hundred more hungry-eyed prospectors arrived.

Ed De La Vergne looked over the boom camp one day and decided money could be made with a townsite. He talked to friends in Colorado Springs and quickly staked out a placer claim of 140 acres around the north and east borders of the Broken Box Ranch where the Carrs lived. This was where he figured the town should be. He had the help of his hired man, Fred Frisbee, Harry Seldomridge from the feed store, and the top four Republican politicians in Colorado Springs. They went together to sign for 20 acres each for a total of 140 acres in one piece. The placer was staked and recorded in the county courthouse. It was all legal. They had 140 acres in what could turn out to be the heart of the town of Cripple Creek. They called it the Hayden Placer.

At once, Dutch Henry's saloon went up near the townsite. The drinking place consisted of little more than a tent with a plank across two beer kegs to serve as a bar. A short time later a tent boarding house was opened by D.C. Williams. An assay shop started business in Squaw Gulch. The Carr ranch house became the center of activity. All emergencies from snakebite to a lost burro brought the people to the Carr's ranch house.

Bob Womack must have watched it with a shock of wonder. He had caused all of this! There were now over eight hundred people in Cripple Creek. It was his gold strike that did it.

He worked now and then on his claim, put his shaft down another six feet, and had a pile of ore stashed in one of the underground tunnels. He still didn't have enough ore to take to Florissant and the railroad. He talked with his miner friends. He went to Colorado Springs again, but no one would finance him so he could work his mine properly.

Even so, this must have been a happy time for Bob. He suddenly had gained respect in the small mining community from both tenderfeet and old-timers. He even had grudging acceptance in Colorado City and the Springs.

In Cripple Creek, tenderfeet often asked him for advice about how to prospect and even how to stake a claim. Soon he spent as much time helping strangers as he did working his own strike. Bob didn't care how much work he got done on his shaft; he didn't have the money to develop it. Anyway, if a man asked you for help, naturally you stopped what you were doing and helped him. It was the neighborly thing to do.

Shortly after the mining district was formed on April 5, George Carr wrote to the owner of the ranch he ran that prospectors were digging up the ranch hunting gold. A few days later Horace Bennett arrived in Cripple Creek to inspect the situation.

He found more activity than he was ready for. He also discovered that some miners and politicians from Colorado Springs had set up a 140-acre "placer claim" that could well be used as a townsite. It was immediately adjacent to his Broken Box ranch. By rushing a land patent through government circles, the Hayden Placer could then be owned by the seven and divided into lots and sold to set up a town.

Bennett knew about land values. It was possible he could do the same thing on the land he owned there. He sent his half brother Melvin Sowle to Cripple Creek to keep an eye on things.

Sowle arrived in Cripple Creek to the whining of sawmills, the pounding of nails, and the loud report of a boomtown gold rush. He found out that the owners of the Hayden Placer were going to sell lots there even before the land was legally theirs by giving a bond that the patent would be granted.

Sowle rushed a report to Bennett suggesting that the ranch be surveyed at once and lots offered for sale.

Bennett stewed over the matter and after a week or more wrote Sowle to go ahead and survey in lots but only on the northern half of the ranch where it was too hilly for good cattle grazing.

The survey was done and the plat filed as "Freemont" on November 6, 1891. The quick survey made no attempt to follow the topography of the area. Many of the lots on the streets could not be sold because of the steep slopes.

The plat was for eighty acres in an oblong. It ran 2,620 feet toward Mount Pisgah, with five streets running north and south for 1,350 feet. They were numbered First through Fifth. The long ones were avenues and named after the founders, Bennett Avenue and Myers Avenue. One was named Carr Avenue after the ranch manager. The others were named Eaton Avenue and Warren Avenue after business acquaintances in Denver.

So the two small towns grew next door to each other as more miners and prospectors stormed into Cripple Creek.

But so far, Cripple Creek was a toothless dragon. Thousands of dollars had been spent prospecting. Some men found upthrusts with real potential, but so far almost no gold ore had been taken from the mines and hauled to the Florissant railroad siding to be sent to a smelter.

It was all expenses and no income. One after another, the miners saw the problems. Many cut back or quit working their claims, and some sold out for $300 to $500.

What was needed was a lifesaver who would validate Cripple Creek as a bona fide investment, one where the right money now could be multiplied a thousand times in a year or two. Many of the miners were in the same fix that Bob Womack was. He had a viable gold mine, but nobody would lend him the money or go into partnership with him to provide the $10,000 to $15,000 to get the mine operating and into a paying proposition.

There had to be some way that the gold mines of Cripple Creek could be shown to be profitable ventures to the men who had the money to invest. Veterans in Cripple Creek knew that if something didn't happen before the snows fell, the boom town of Cripple Creek might not last out the winter.

CHAPTER 4

Development Money Cometh

While Cripple Creek struggled through the tough summer of 1891, the man who would save the day was in Colorado Springs with problems of his own. Count James Pourtales had arrived in the Springs in 1885 with two purposes: to marry his French cousin who was a heartbreaker and beautiful, and to make money to help save the historic family estate in the Silesian section of Germany.

He was a real German Count and lord of nine Silesian villages and the family estate called Glumbowitz.

He soon married his cousin, who had been sent to Florissant by her family to live with her brother, away from French society and the evils of strong drink. Pourtales and his beautiful bride made a splash in the Springs high society. Then the Count settled down to making money.

He took over a failing dairy farm and turned it into a moneymaker, then planned his big venture. He would build a large casino and resort and lake on part of the dairy farm near Cheyenne Mountain and make millions offering roulette and other gambling games to the swells and the international playboy set that peopled Colorado Springs.

Count Pourtales borrowed $250,000 from friends in London and New York and with his Germanic efficiency designed and built the casino and offered lots for sale around the lake. The splashy casino opened in June of 1891 and prospered for a week before General Palmer, the man who established HIS town of Colorado Springs, showed his disapproval. He evidently talked to county officials, and all sorts of violations were quickly discovered, and the resort and the roulette wheel and the whole complex closed down.

The Count found himself in a financial crunch. His backers for the casino were making noises, and a sizable mortgage would be due soon on the estate in Germany. He began looking for new sources of income.

One day in August of 1891 he shared a table with Ed De La Vergne in the El Paso Club in the Springs. Ed was full of talk about Cripple Creek and the problems there.

De La Vergne told the Count that almost every day somebody else uncovered an upthrust of gold out there at Cripple Creek. By that day there must have been two or three dozen proven gold strikes.

The Count said that must mean there were a lot of rich men in Cripple Creek.

Ed told him that in reality most of the men were almost broke and several prospectors had sold their claims for $300. He explained that it takes money, lots of it, to turn a proven upthrust with a vein of gold in it into a paying gold mine. Most of the mines needed about $25,000 to get started.

The Count noted that there were lots of rich men in Colorado Springs. He asked why they didn't finance the gold mines.

De La Vergne said that nobody would believe the gold strike was real because of the gold mine hoaxes that had flourished around the Springs. Ed said that he could almost guarantee that a $25,000 investment now could result in a return of a thousand-to-one within two years.

Things were getting desperate out at the digs. If something didn't happen soon out there, the Cripple Creek gold rush might turn into a total disaster—all because nobody would invest in proven mines to get the gold out of the ground.

The Count became interested, and the two men talked through the afternoon. Ed must have been at his persuasive best, telling the Count about how Bob Womack found the first upthrust, and now he and dozens of other miners had proven gold veins but no cash to turn them into producing mines.

The next day Count Pourtales looked up his good friend, Thomas C. Parrish, who had done a lot of prospecting himself. The Count told him about Cripple Creek and what Ed De La Vergne had told him. Ed was a member of the upper society class in the Springs, and his word carried a lot of weight. Parrish listened closely and when the Count finished, the rich man was convinced. He said he'd known Ed for several years and that Ed knew as much about gold mining as any man in the Springs. Parrish told the Count that if the gold was lying there waiting to be taken, they should do something about it. They arranged to take a ride out to Cripple Creek and see for themselves.

A week later, about the middle of August, Parrish led Count Pourtales on a horseback ride to Cripple Creek up the Cheyenne Mountain trail. They arrived at the Broken Box ranch house.

Emma Carr liked the polite, flattering big German, and he and Parrish stayed with the Carrs while they investigated the Cripple Creek strikes.

They began their tour. Bob Womack took them to Battle Mountain to talk to William Scott Stratton about the financing problems for the miners. Stratton told them they should go look at Steve Blair's shaft, the Buena Vista, on the north side of Bull Hill.

They investigated the claim and the shaft and liked what they saw. The two continued their survey, even staking placer claims in places and taking carefully labeled samples of ore for assay later in the Springs.

The Count and Parrish did a thorough job studying the holes and claims and the land of Cripple Creek. They toured the area through September, and then late in October they said good-bye to the many friends they had made among the miners and headed back for the Springs.

Bob Womack and Ed De La Vergne agreed that the miners had just lost another chance to get some financing. Ed figured that the Count still had some money or he could raise it. They both knew about the quarter of a million dollars the Count had borrowed from friends in London and New York to start his failed casino.

But the two decided that the Count would be like the others, wanting a sure-fire investment.

Ed was especially saddened by the financing problem, since he couldn't even convince his own brother in the Springs to invest in his mine.

Bob Womack told Ed that if they didn't get some kind of money action by the time the real snow hit Cripple Creek, they all might as well pack up their goods and head for warmer climates.

Back in the Springs, Count Pourtales was busy arranging financing. He had been convinced about the wealth underground in Cripple Creek.

On November 10, 1891 the news broke in the Springs paper. Count Pourtales had purchased Steve Blair's Buena

Vista claim and mine in Cripple Creek for $80,000. The Count was quoted in the newspaper as saying that he had seen more than a million dollars worth of gold in the Buena Vista, and there was probably much more there.

When the Springs newspapers reached Cripple Creek late that afternoon on the stage from Florissant, they created an immediate sensation.

Ed De La Vergne read the story and tears ran down his cheeks. Ed knew that this was what the town needed. To have the Count put up his money would trigger other big money in the Springs. The Count's prestige and social standing and his reliability would bring a rush of people to look at the mines.

The story went on that the Count said that the Cripple Creek District had at least a hundred other mines and claims that were as valuable as the Buena Vista.

There was an immediate reaction. The next day engineers began arriving from the Springs, from Denver, Aspen, Pueblo, and even Canon City to check out the mines and their potential. These were heady times. The money men were coming.

Every day news broke that another claim had been sold or that the owner had bargained for financing on a partnership basis so the real production could begin.

A month before, Winfield Scott Stratton had tried in vain in the Springs to sell his Washington claim for $500. Now with the big money men sniffing around, his price went up and he soon sold it for $80,000.

About this time, one of the strangest events took place in all of mining history. Bob Womack owned half of the El Paso claim with his partner Dr. Grannis. Some say that Bob went on a drinking spree to celebrate the good fortune of Cripple Creek and the fact that at last the big money needed for working the vast wealth was at hand. They say that while Bob was in a highly intoxicated state, he offered to sell his half of the El Paso claim for a ridiculously low amount.

Some say that Bob had burned himself out, that he was filled to the brim with gold mining and prospecting and coaching the tenderfeet, and that he simply wanted out of the mining business.

Now and then someone will bring up the idea that Bob Womack was a pioneer, a discoverer, a man who would spend twelve years of hardship, poverty, heartbreak, and ultimate ridicule and teasing as "Crazy" Bob Womack in two towns, so he could eventually prove that he was right and that he had found the first strike in the Cripple Creek gold field. Once he had proven his point, he lost interest in the project.

The facts known are that Bob Womack sold his 50 percent interest in the El Paso claim to his partner, Dr. Grannis, for $300.

These were big money days. Bob Womack must have known that the mine was worth many, many times the $300. His friend Stratton had sold his Washington claim for $80,000. Didn't this interest him? He must have seen dozens of other claims no better than his sell for many thousands of dollars.

Why did he duck and run for $300?

No one will ever know.

There is a theory that Bob Womack was afraid of wealth, that he wouldn't know what to do with a thousand dollars, or a hundred thousand dollars. He backed away and avoided the problem of wealth by selling out to his partner.

A mild support for this idea comes from Bob himself, who had left Cripple Creek after an illness and learned that William Scott Stratton was Cripple Creek's first millionaire. Bob was sad for a moment, then he flashed a big smile. "Poor Old Man Stratton," Bob said. "All that money to worry about. . . . I don't envy him one bit."

Some say that Bob Womack was a prospector, not a miner. He did not want the responsibility of managing other men's lives, of running a hard rock mine, of taking on the task of financing, of keeping the books, or hiring people, or worrying about all the investments, dealing with stocks on the open market for the mine, and the thousand and one other things that he would need to do to be a partner in a mine with the dentist.

One of the most perplexing problems with the sale of the El Paso to Dr. Grannis is the morality of the dentist. Why would he even consider accepting half of a potentially million dollar property for $300? He had worked and struggled and risked a great deal along with Bob to find this gold mine. Why would he then accept such an offer? Was it true that Bob was liquored up and sold the El Paso on a whim and had regretted it the next day? Why would Dr. Grannis even think of taking such an offer seriously from a drunken partner?

Shortly after the deal with Bob Womack, Dr. Grannis sold four fifths of the El Paso to Claire Frisbee for $8,000. Claire's husband was Fred Frisbee, who had been working with Old Man Stratton.

Fred Frisbee was furious with his wife, but before he could vent his anger, she promptly sold three fifths of the El Paso to the coal dealer in the Springs, William Lennox, for $8,000. Claire thus still owned her remaining one fifth of the El Paso claim at no cost to herself. Not too much later Judge Colburn, from the Springs, bought a tenth interest in the El Paso claim for $10,000.

There Bob Womack sat with his $300 and no interest whatsoever in the El Paso claim.

When the years had passed and the big gold mining days were over in Cripple Creek, the El Paso mine had taken out slightly over $3 million in gold. Absolutely none of it went to the founder of the Cripple Creek gold rush, Bob Womack.

The flow of money into Cripple Creek continued. Claims that proved out were financed or sold and good times rolled. The two men who started the money flow had come on hard times. Count Pourtales and Parrish had exhausted their money tree and couldn't find anyone to finance the development of their Buena Vista claim.

Then the Pharmacist claim on Bull Hill, owned by Springs drugstore owners A. D. Jones and J.K. Miller, hit a vein that assayed out at $510 a ton. Word spread quickly.

Count Pourtales knew this was his big chance. He got some of the high grade ore and took it to the Springs and showed it to one of the richest men in town, James J. Hagerman.

His sales pitch must have gone something like this: This ore comes from the Pharmacist mine just 400 yards from my Buena Vista mine. Some of the same kind of ore is undoubtedly in the Buena Vista.

Hagerman was interested but not convinced. He sent for Wolcott Newberry, a top mining engineer, who ran Hagerman's Mollie Gibson silver mine in Aspen. Newberry inspected the Buena Vista and agreed that some of the same veins in the Pharmacist probably were present in the Buena Vista. It was a viable mining prospect.

Hagerman opened his wallet and took out $225,000 to develop the Buena Vista mine and to buy up twenty-one other Bull Hill claims. He called the group the Isabella Gold Mining Company.

Hagerman knew what he was doing. The Isabella company took out $15.7 million worth of gold from Bull Hill.

By the end of 1891 there were 450 residents in Cripple Creek. It was beginning to look like a town. Many of the tents had been replaced by wooden buildings. The days of growth, grandeur, and glory lay just ahead.

CHAPTER 5

Two Struggling Townsites

As the winter snows swirled around the two new townsites in the Cripple Creek Mining District at the start of 1892, both seemed to be prospering. The town of Fremont, platted by Bennett and Meyers, perched on seventy-nine hilly acres in a rough rectangle laid out east to west.

The sister town of Hayden Placer was on 140 acres of land and structured in a north-south direction adjacent to Fremont. Both emerging municipalities competed for businesses and residents, but Hayden Placer had one large problem. All deeds in Hayden Placer had stipulations that prevented the use of any lots for gambling or saloons.

A mining boomtown without gambling, saloons, and whores? Soon the business firms including the gaming houses and drinking establishments began their businesses in Fremont, where no such restrictions were in force. That left Hayden Placer to cater more to the residential type of construction.

In Fremont there were 776 lots, all 25 feet wide and 125 feet long. The first prices on lots were twenty-five dollars for inside and fifty dollars for corner lots.

The first business firms to set up shop in Fremont were a barber and a saloon. Pete Hettig and Robert Work were the first enterprising businessmen. The barbershop was in a tent and the saloon consisted solely of a plank laid across two beer kegs for a bar in the great outdoors.

The Hayden Placer was not officially platted until February 15, 1892, but the promoters had been selling lots with the assurance that it would be official soon. They had 140 acres and laid out 1,320 lots.

EARLY ON IN CRIPPLE CREEK, tents with platforms and floors like this one became a quick way to put up a working office. Here the town's first "court house" is good enough for the Justice of the Peace and Charles H. Adams, Attorney At Law. (Photo Courtesy Colorado Springs Pioneer Museum)

Tents worked fine for a time, but what was needed was lumber to build houses and stores. Soon there were eight local sawmills operating in the area to supply raw lumber for the new buildings. There was no time to let the freshly cut green lumber cure, and it was often cut down, taken to the mill, sawed into one-by-sixes and two-by-fours, and nailed into place in a building in Fremont or Hayden Placer during the same day. This led in a few months to cracks between the boards when they dried out and shrank to permanent size.

Wooden buildings soon replaced the tents along the main street of Bennett Avenue in Fremont. Along with the saloons, dance halls, gambling halls, and "houses for the ladies of the evening," other firms quickly sprang up to serve the fast-growing towns. Some of the first were the general stores, grocery stores, and restaurants to provide food. Even 450 people eat a lot, and the newly formed freight and passenger line from the railroad depot at Florissant to the Cripple Creek Mining District soon hauled as much foodstuffs as it did people.

Construction in the newly formed towns was primitive but effective. Usually it was unpainted wooden clapboards with the boards nailed up vertically. When cracks appeared between boards, they were covered with thin strips of boards called batting. Old newspapers were used for insulation inside with burlap often pasted over the insulation or over the vertical boards. Tent canvas was often used in place of a ceiling of wood. Slanted boards usually made up the roof, with corrugated iron on the more expensive buildings. Often rafters were boarded over to form attics for the children to sleep in or for storage.

At the start, the store owners lived in the back or in a loft over their firms. By the end of 1892 many felt secure enough to put up separate houses.

After a year, lots in the two townsites that sold for $25 had risen in price to $250. A modest cabin-type house could be put up for $500. If you could find a house to rent, it would cost you about $15 a month.

All of the businesses and houses had privies since there was no indoor plumbing and no piped-in water. Water sold for fifty cents a barrel or five cents a bucket.

By the spring of 1892 electricity had arrived in the townsites. It was produced by a coal-fired generator. Tall poles along main street held carbon-arc lights. The same summer of 1892 telephone service was established in town and with Colorado Springs, and telegraph lines were extended from the railroad at Florissant to Cripple Creek.

Law enforcement in the two townsites was almost non-existent. One El Paso County deputy sheriff from Colorado Springs marched up and down the two small towns representing the law. His name was Peter Eales and he had little to do.

Many of the residents were from Colorado Springs and not the usual goldrush thieves, killers, hard women, and cheats. This fact is borne out since the first killing in the Cripple Creek District wasn't until April of 1892 when Charles Huespeth, an ex-convict, tried to kill a bartender in the Ironclad Dance Hall. His revolver shot missed him and killed Reuben Miller, the piano player.

Much of the lawman's first duties involved settling fist fights in saloons and brothels and checking the prostitutes to be sure they were paying their head tax and making regular contributions to area churches.

By the summer of 1892 there were 150 business firms in the two small townsites. These included forty restaurants and boarding houses, seven hotels, six mining and hardware supply stores, four meat markets, seventeen real estate offices, two drug stores, a wagon shop, and twenty-five saloons. The houses of prostitution were not counted as businesses.

By this time the number of residents in the side-by-side towns had risen to almost 2,000, and some reported that there were fifty mines now shipping out gold ore to the mills. The two small towns had a few officials but no municipal services whatsoever. There were no taxes either, and the two side-by-side towns struggled through 1892 with duplicate mayors and councilmen and a growing thrill of discovery and gold mining which was central to all parties concerned.

The first large hotel to be built in the area was the Continental in Fremont. The two stories contained forty rooms. They advertised that they could accommodate 200 people, which meant five persons to a room or they had to sleep on the dining room tables and in the hallways.

Hayden Place had its own hotel in April of 1892 on the corner of Bison and Pike's Peak, the Clarendon. It had 125 rooms, a dining hall that could seat 100, stagecoach offices, and a ladies' parlor that sported a grand piano and a billiard room. A few months after the opening, the Clarendon put in electric lights, a fire alarm system, and the wonder of the day, hot and cold running water in the rooms.

A town has to have a mayor and officials, and both Fremont and Hayden's Placer had them, working side by side.

Fremont's first election was a race between George Carr and Peter Hettig. Carr won by a big margin, but before the ballots could be given a verified count, some of Hettig's backers had a game of catch with several shoeboxes of ballots. The ballots became lost, strayed, and mangled, and no count could be taken.

A new election was called and George Carr ran against Dr. John A. Whiting. Again Carr was the overwhelming favorite; after all he and his wife Emma had done favors for and given food and lodging to half the men in the camp.

But Carr and his election manager, Bob Womack, imbibed of strong drink one night before the election and later lassoed the leaders of Whiting's campaign and dragged them playfully through the streets.

The proper and law-abiding members of the town decided that Carr was a bit too wild to be mayor and elected their doctor as the first mayor.

Bennett Avenue slowly became the "main street" of Fremont, with stores and shops, groceries and hardware, and mining equipment stores. Some of the specialty shops were equal to any found in that day in Denver.

In the summer of 1891 a sudden flurry of talk swept through the small mining community. Blanche Barton had moved her business operations from Colorado City to Cripple Creek, believing that there were enough men there that her services would be in demand. She set up her business in a small red-striped tent not far from Bob Womack's shack in Poverty Gulch. Blanche had been popular in Colorado Springs at the going rate of two dollars a fling. She was a big woman for the day at five-eight, had flowing henna red hair, soft blue eyes, and breasts described as "the size of pumpkins." By August business had been so good that she moved into a wooden house.

As the Cripple Creek Mining District's first whore, Blanche did well. Her price began at five dollars the first week and then soon went up to fifteen dollars in August. But with the addition of a house with six girls in Fremont, she had to lower her price to meet the competition. It soon leveled out at four dollars a turn.

One day Blanche came to Bob Womack with a small problem. Bob had known her professionally, and she believed him to be a clear thinker and honest in all things.

She told Bob that she had a friend who she did truly admire. He'd been running a little short of cash and had been paying her with some slips of paper. Blanche admitted that she didn't read "none too good" and asked Bob to look at the slips and tell her what they said.

She stood at the door to Bob's shack, and he came out and sat in his favorite rocking chair on the little porch overlooking Cripple Creek.

She held out a handful of small pieces of paper, some on lined stock, some from a torn-off sack, some on writing paper. Each one of the slips said the same thing. Bob read them:

"I, Tim Hussey, owe Blanche Barton a one-eighth share in my hard rock mining claim, the Prince Albert in the Cripple Creek Mining District."

One of them was dated June 10, 1891 and signed in a bold scrawl with "Tim Hussey."

Tim was a drinking buddy and longtime friend who had been prospecting around Cripple Creek from the start and was a solid companion of Womack.

Bob asked the party girl how many of the slips she had. She didn't know so they counted them. Blanche owned twenty-seven one-eighth shares of Tim's claim.

Nobody knows what Blanche did with her I.O.U.'s from Tim Hussey. He had been there at the start and saw his claim through to the development of the Prince Albert mine. Nobody knows if she confronted him with the fact that she owned his claim and his mine three and a half times over. In the summer of 1893 some slick promoters and fancy lawyers swindled Tim Hussey out of his mine. The shock of losing what he had worked and struggled so hard for over so many years took its toll on Tim. He lost his mind and disappeared from the Cripple Creek scene.

Every town needs a newspaper, and Cripple Creek area had its first one early. In December of 1891 E.C. Gard moved his newspapering plant from Palmer Lake and set it up in a log cabin in Cripple Creek. He named the paper the *Cripple Creek Crusher*. The first edition came out with gilt-laden ink.

The *Crusher* published until January of 1895 when it was sold by Gard and came out under the name *Cripple Creek Times*.

During the summer of 1892 competition increased among the stores, and the owners began to make their buildings more pleasing to the eye to help draw in customers.

Galvanized steel became the rule for the best firms. Shiplap type horizontal boards replaced the vertical ones, and more and more windows went into the store fronts to make them more attractive and to show off the wares.

Often awnings were hung over the store fronts. New buildings now had ornate trim work on them including cornices, parapets, and other architectural niceties that had nothing to do with the practical aspects that had held sway a year before.

Houses began to show improvements as well. As the money began to come to Cripple Creek in the form of wages, and receipts at stores, the homes began to look better. They had porches with trim work, curtains at the windows, even a bay window here and there.

At first the several churches in town had been held in upstairs areas over business firms and saloons. Now they could afford to move out and put up structures of their own.

With all the improvements there were still two necessities that any town needs and both Hayden Placer and Fremont still lacked: there was no piped-in water and no sewer system.

Both towns had contemplated such moves and had made starts at the projects, but the task was complicated and out of the financial reach of both the small communities.

For some time there had been a movement about to consolidate the two settlements into one. At last the proponents won out in both towns, and a measure was put on a special ballot to combine the two under one administration and a new name.

On February 23 the ballot measure passed, and Fremont and Hayden Placer were merged into a new town with the official name of Cripple Creek.

Now the work on the sewer and the water mains went ahead in earnest; there was enough tax money so it could be done.

The town grew in many ways. Those who came there were not the get-rich-quick type that peopled the placer strikes where the gold had been washed down into streams and river beds and lay there on the surface, in riffles, or ten feet underground ready to be panned out and taken to town.

This was hard rock country, where the start was slow, but the length of stay might be twenty years before the veins of gold deep into the mountain were worked out. This type of miner was more stable, often with a family and hopes and dreams that could be accomplished.

There were no gold mines sprouting in the middle of Cripple Creek, although some did show up in the middle of the town of Victor nearby in the same mining district. There were no streets torn up when an old stream bed was found to run under it and the stream bed was worth a thousand dollars a foot in placer gold as happened in some placer strikes.

In Cripple Creek the town had been laid out systematically by surveyors, lots formed and sold, streets specified, and the main avenues set at eighty feet across.

As these law-abiding, honest, hard-working miners assembled and went to work, the town of Cripple Creek and those small towns surrounding it that grew up became more settled, more up-to-date, more sophisticated. The town of Cripple Creek was established, growing, and here for the long run.

Those first few years, one of the major events in Cripple Creek was the arrival of the stagecoach from Florissant. The stage and freight wagons were the lifeline of the fledging town, bringing in everything from the outside world that could be shipped on a railroad freight car and a freight wagon. It all showed up in Cripple Creek's shops and stores.

For years idlers and watchers and just plain folks waited at the stage depot, whether it was at some store or later at the front steps of the Continental Hotel, to catch the arrival of the charging team of six and the stagecoach as it roared into town.

Alonzo Welty had the first stage lines in those wonder days of Cripple Creek in 1891 and into '92. His rickety wagons with cow ponies struggled up the last ridge before Cripple Creek and then came flying down the slope into town with a flourish befitting any stagecoach arrival in the Old West in Wyoming or Dodge City or Arizona.

One of the watchers often was Bob Womack, who had sold out his claim and now loafed about town. The arrival of the stage brought new people, new fashions, word of the outside world, and newspapers from Colorado Springs, Denver, Chicago, and even the *New York Times*, if someone cared to subscribe.

Welty's wagons were soon replaced by John Hundley's Antler's Livery from the Springs. The trip from the rail siding in Florissant to the booming gold mine camp was eighteen miles. The coaches made one stop, that at the Welty ranch house on Four Mile.

The cowboy horses Welty had used had been traded in for bigger, stronger animals that pulled the stages. Hundley's drivers were instructed never to strain or overtire the horses. They often took their time hauling the heavy stages up the last hill to Cripple Creek.

Once on the top with the mining town laid out before them, the horses were often given some time to rest. Then the driver would shout to the passengers to hold on to anything they could find.

The driver cracked his whip, and the horses plunged down the hill toward Cripple Creek. The coach was on the last short leg into town. It thundered past the cemetery, rounded the corners, and rushed up the Cripple Creek streets until the driver jumped on the brakes with both feet, bringing the coach to a dust raising stop in front of the Continental Hotel or some other stage depot that was designated over the years.

Cripple Creek soon built churches. More than 30 percent of the residents of the town were Irish Catholics. Bishop Matz of Denver sent a young priest named Father Volpe to organize a Catholic church.

The Rev. Horace Sanderson, a Bostonian Congregationalist, beat the Catholics for first church in town honors when he set up a large framed tent on Carr Avenue and called it the Whosover Will Congregational Church. It was used for civic and social functions as well until a building of adequate size was constructed in the community.

During the first two years, Cripple Creek's production of gold had gone from zero to $50,000 a month, then to $100,000. Near the end of 1893 it rose to over $200,000 a month. By January of 1894 the population of Cripple Creek was set at just over 12,500. The gold rush that Bob Womack had started had turned the high mountain cauldron of an old volcano into a true hardrock boomtown, and this was only the start.

CHAPTER 6

Bob Womack in Deep Clover

After Bob Womack gave up his half interest in the El Paso mine for $300, he spent his time working at what he knew best. He still helped out the tenderfeet who kept flocking to town. He took great satisfaction that he was still known as "the man who started the whole thing" there at Cripple Creek.

As the tenderfeet increased and men turned from prospecting to working in the mines, there was less interest in him as the discoverer of the Cripple Creek Bonanza.

Bob began waiting for the daily stagecoaches to arrive in town at the depot wherever it happened to be. He was constantly amazed at the interesting and sometimes famous people who stepped off the stage. In the early days there were sons of rich men who sent the boys to Cripple Creek with a $10,000 poke and told them to find a mine and make themselves rich. At least two of them did.

There were writers and politicians and housewives and men looking to work in the deep rock mines. A cross section of working-class America came down the steps of the stage-coach, and Bob Womack was there to watch and wonder.

Bob seemed busier than ever. He had no time to find another claim, to stake another mine. He was always welcome in the saloons and cafes of Cripple Creek, and there almost never was any pay needed. Someone would be willing to buy him a drink or a dinner to listen to him talk about the early days, only a year or two ago, of Cripple Creek.

Bob stayed away from the Sunshine Ranch that his sister Miss Lida still ran for her father. He had more important things to do.

Poker was one. He loved the game and often got into three-day sessions with some of his old-time buddies such as Tim Hussey, Melvin Sowle, and Jimmie Burns.

While the mine owners developed their properties into multimillion-dollar bonanzas, Bob Womack stood back and watched, apparently glad that he wasn't caught up in the frantic manipulations of the stock market where shares in Cripple Creek mines were sold and traded on the street before the new stock exchange was built.

Bob wasn't the only one in town to sell out his mine for a ridiculously low price. Bob felt a kinship with some of these other men and spent a lot of time with them. These prospectors who had sold their rich mines for a drink or a poker ante included Lafe Fyffe, Joe Whalen, and Horace Barry. The four of them had located dozens of Cripple Creek's best claims and frittered them away without any good reason.

As 1892 turned into 1893, there were fewer and fewer men who asked where they could find Bob Womack. The new flood of prospectors and miners weren't interested in Bob; they wanted to find a rich mine or go to work in one.

Bob worked his circuit of saloons and cafes and restaurants, drank too much, talked too much, and spent time with his friends from the old days who had no more to do than Bob did.

Toward the end of 1893 Bob was drinking more than he was eating. He lost a lot of weight and had a series of coughing spells and colds. A week before Christmas 1893, Bob caught another cold and it developed into pneumonia. He took to his bed.

Poverty gulch had become the far end of Meyers Avenue and the low-priced end of the string of cribs and whorehouses. One of the madams who had a small house near Bob's shack liked Bob, and when she heard he was sick she sent her girls to his side to nurse him around the clock. Milda James was the softhearted Negro madam, and her medicine for Bob was a tablespoon of kerosene every two hours.

Either the kerosene cured Bob, or he hated taking it so much that he willed himself well. He recovered. Pneumonia in those days was a killer, and Bob marveled at his good luck to still be alive.

His sickness changed his lifestyle. No longer did he get together with his hard-drinking companions. He left the cafe circuit to the miners who were bringing in one bonanza after another.

On December 24, 1893, Bob sold his Womack Placer claim for $500 and changed the money into one dollar bills. This was in a time when a gold miner worked nine hours underground for three dollars a day.

On Christmas Day Bob walked down the chilly streets to Third and Bennett. It was the busiest intersection in town. There he began giving out a dollar bill to every child who passed.

The word spread quickly and kids came from all sides and got in line. Soon the kids seemed to be taller, and Bob took a closer look. He realized that a lot of men were getting into the line, taking the dollar, and then going back in line for seconds.

Bob waited for the next oversized kid with whiskers and belted him one with his fist. The miner took the blow and swung his own fist at Bob, knocking him to the sidewalk.

The money giveaway was over.

Bob's old friend, saloon keeper Johnnie Nolan, picked up Bob, and Deputy Sheriff Pete Eales carried him back to his shack in Poverty Gulch. The deputy sent a wire to Marshal Dana in Colorado Springs, and he had a deputy ride out to Sunview Ranch and tell Miss Lida.

Bob's sister left everything and rode to the Springs and took the train to Florissant, where she rode the stage and arrived at Bob's shack the afternoon of December 26.

Miss Lida made some soup that she said would get him well in no time.

Bob was despondent and felt he had nothing to live for. He threatened to get well enough so he could walk and then find a hundred-foot-deep mine shaft he could jump into.

Miss Lida made the soup and stood over Bob while he ate all of it. He needed some food in his system as much as anything. Having Miss Lida there was part of the cure. The soup made him feel better, and that afternoon Bob was almost his old self, laughing and joking with Miss Lida.

She sat down and had a long talk with Bob. She told him that she'd been selling off pieces of the Sunview Ranch. She said their Pa was too old to do anything, and she was getting tired of cattle. She told Bob she had about decided to sell the rest of the homestead and use the money to buy a house in the Springs. Not a fancy place but a big one where she could set up a room and board business.

Miss Lida told him she wanted him to go to the Springs and be partners with her in the boardinghouse. She needed a handyman around the place to help take care of things.

She even had a house spotted on Cascade Avenue that would be about right for them.

After the talk and the rest and more soup later that day, Bob made up his mind. He was done in Cripple Creek and it was time he moved on. He warmed to the idea of living in the Springs and having a boardinghouse.

On December 27, 1893, Bob Womack asked Melvin Sowle to rent his shack on Poverty Gulch, and he and Miss Lida took the stage for Florissant.

A few weeks later Miss Lida and Bob opened their boardinghouse at 703 North Cascade Avenue in the Springs. Bob gained back much of the weight he had lost. But despite his best intentions, the life-long quest for gold got the best of him and the fever struck him again. He took short prospecting trips into the small camps that seemed to blossom almost weekly in the West Pikes Peak area around Cripple Creek. Nothing came of any of his trips.

They became fewer and fewer the more Bob became fascinated with the boardinghouse. Soon Bob took to cooking and did much of the work when Miss Lida was otherwise occupied. He gave himself the title of Number Two Cook and wore big white aprons.

Bob enjoyed his new calling. He baked biscuits, kept the woodbox filled for the big kitchen range, and washed dishes. He was happy and contented working around the house.

He heard about the big strikes and rich veins that the miners in Cripple Creek were finding. Now and then Bob took a visit to Cripple Creek, but he never stayed. His contacts with the invalids in the boardinghouse made Bob think about his own health and his hard drinking. He made up his mind quickly and got one more "grubstake" from Miss Lida and went to Denver to "take the Keeley cure."

This cure for alcoholism was promoted by Dr. Leslie E. Keeley and was used all across the United States in those times. It included injections of bichloride of gold into the patient's veins and drinking raw carrot juice. Besides the medicine, the cure used a benevolent system of concern and helpful attention. Bob took the cure in Denver, returned to the boardinghouse, and didn't have another drink of whiskey for as long as he lived.

Soon he didn't go back to Cripple Creek anymore, becoming involved totally in the boardinghouse and the people there. He watched and listened to the success of Cripple Creek and must have had a warm feeling, knowing that he started it all. Without him there still might not have been a dollar's worth of gold taken out of Cripple Creek, the greatest bonanza of them all.

TRAFFIC JAM IN Cripple Creek in 1893: big rigs, small buggies, and even mules towing wagons. This is the Great Gold Bank, but the bank is hard to find. Maybe all of those wagons are loaded with gold to deposit. Maybe not. Traffic hasn't improved much. (Photo Courtesy Colorado Springs Pioneer Museum)

CHAPTER 7

Striking it Rich

An old saying goes: "Gold is where you find it," and that certainly applied in the Cripple Creek Bonanza. In the thirty-six square miles of the Cripple Creek volcanic cauldron, gold showed up in totally unexpected places.

In the early days, Bob Womack had worked for twelve years to locate the first upthrust and the first mine, the El Paso. In 1893 one tenderfoot who knew nothing at all about mines, gold or otherwise, simply threw his hat in the air. Where it fell is where he staked out his claim, and on that spot he dug down and discovered an upthrust and his gold mine.

The Buena Vista with Count Pourtales' help had been the kick-starter for the big money men and was nearing production. Good quality ore came out of the Pharmacist mine. Things were picking up in the gold fields.

Winfield Scott Stratton had disdained the usual areas where most of the miners staked out claims. He thought that Bob Womack's Poverty Gulch and Gold Hill were not the best of sites for a real bonanza. Bull Hill off to the east of Gold Hill didn't seem to be a productive area either.

He chose Battle Mountain a mile south of Bull Hill because he figured that it was on the south rim of the ancient volcano's cauldron and should be rich in ore.

The layout of the area is something like this. Battle Mountain covers about 500 acres and tops out at 10,300 feet. Bull Hill stood higher at 10,800 feet a mile north of Battle. To the south lay Squaw Mountain. Over Squaw Mountain northwest was Raven Hill. A mile northwest of Raven Hill you came to Gold Hill. The village of Cripple Creek lay just below Gold Hill.

On Battle Mountain the Black Diamond under J.R. McKinnie's direction had started producing good paying ore. Nearby the Strong mine owned by Sam Strong had hit a worthwhile vein.

Three Irishmen will forever be a part of the legends of Cripple Creek's bonanza because of the strange turn they took to becoming millionaires. Jimmie Burns was an old-timer at Cripple Creek, arriving shortly after Winfield Scott Stratton did in 1891. He tramped the hills searching. He had staked some worthless claims, and he tagged along with Stratton one time until the small man with the white hair became angry with him and sent him packing.

Jimmie Burns and his partner, Jimmie Doyle, followed Stratton's move to Battle Mountain and staked a claim above Stratton's Independence. Nothing came of it. They were impressed by Stratton's confidence that the south slope of Battle Mountain must be rich in gold ore. The Irish partners toured the area but found it already staked with no room for new claims.

Part of the reason the area was already claimed was the presence of two placer claims of 160 acres each. One was the Mount Rosa Placer staked by J.R. McKinnie in 1891. In

January of the next year, M.S. Raynolds platted the Victor C. Adams homestead where he hoped to build a town to be called Lawrence.

McKinnie watched the surveyors and figured that his own land would be better for a townsite than the Adams homestead. To make it more realistic, he shifted his claim stakes south a little over a hundred feet so his south property lines met and matched the north line of the Lawrence site.

Other miners watched the operation and saw a chance to move their claim stakes several dozen feet to the south as well so they would be closer to Stratton's claims. Most figured that Stratton was the guiding star to mining in Cripple Creek and knew what he was doing.

All of this juggling of boundaries brought little interest from Doyle and Burns. Then one day Doyle was walking over the area northwest of the Independence claim. He checked on the moved stakes, and to his surprise he found that the moving of stakes had left a "splinter" of unclaimed land right in the middle of the whole thing.

Doyle didn't waste any time. He drove his stakes into the fragment of Battle Mountain and filed with the county under the names of Burns and Doyle and named the claim the Portland, which had been home to him and Jimmie Burns in Maine.

When the survey was completed, Burns and Doyle found out that they had the grand total of 69/1000 of an acre or about .07 acre. It was roughly 3,000 square feet. It indeed was a splinter.

The two Irishmen dug a hole, putting down a shaft ten feet as was required to maintain their claim, and then began arguing who should do the most work in the hole. Both were frustrated and impatient, wishing that they had a paying mine but not knowing much about the process. Both later admitted that they hadn't the slightest idea what gold ore looked like or how to find it.

They kept blasting and digging, lifting the rock and dirt out of the shaft with a windlass bucket. After two weeks they had a shaft thirty feet down but still had found nothing that proved to them they had a gold mine.

One day Jimmie Burns climbed out of the hole, tired, dirty, and wondering if he had done a sane thing coming to Cripple Creek. He spotted a man he knew walking toward the dig. He called to John Harnan, another Irishman.

Harnan came over and the two talked. Doyle came up and soon the conversation came around to the claim and the hole.

Harnan had been working with gold ore since he was a teenager. He had been sorting ore at the Stratton Independence mine for weeks. His brother had located a bonanza called Hilltop near Fairplay.

In colorful language Doyle told the man that they were getting a mite out of sorts about the hole in the ground they owned. He explained that they were down thirty feet and hadn't found a vein or anything. But he admitted that he wasn't sure he'd know what a gold vein looked like if it whacked him alongside his Irish head.

They talked a bit more, and Harnan looked at the Portland dump where the partners had deposited the buckets full of dirt and rocks they hauled up out of their hole.

Harnan must not have believed his eyes but didn't let on. At the top of one of the piles in the dump was a large chunk of sylvanite. . . .telluride of gold, valuable gold bearing ore.

Harnan asked if it would be helping the lads if he went down the shaft and took a wee look at what they had done so far. The other two Irishmen nodded and showed him to the ladder.

Before his head vanished down the hole, Harnan stopped and looked at the Irish partners and asked them what they would give him if he could find a gold vein down the shaft. Jimmie Burns swore that if Harnan could find gold in that worthless hole, they would give him a third interest in their claim. Doyle quickly agreed. At that point the partners had absolutely nothing to lose.

Harnan went down the wooden ladder, inspecting the sides of the hole as he went. He got to the bottom and called up for the partners to move the ladder to the other side of the shaft.

Once that was done, Harnan began to check out the side of the hole that had been covered by the ladder. Halfway up he spotted the telltale signs of sylvanite in a good-sized vein of gold ore. He invited the two Jimmies down for a look.

The partnership was struck, and a week later the three men had a drift working along the vein of sylvanite and stored the gold ore in gunny sacks.

Harnan warned them that they must be close-mouthed about what they had found. Not a word about it to anyone. He reminded them that they didn't have a full ten-acre claim. He asked them if they had ever heard of the law of apex.

The fledging mine owners hadn't.

Harnan explained to them that the law of apex meant that whoever owns the land where a gold vein comes to the surface is the one who owns the vein. This vein hadn't surfaced. They had broken into it on its way up or down. The point was it didn't come to the surface on the legal site of the Portland claim. If they let the word leak out that they had a horizontal vein, all of the owners of the land surrounding them were going to sue them and claim that the vein was theirs because that vein could come to the surface on their claim.

Chapter 7

Jimmie Burns asked Harnan for advice, and the experienced miner told then first they should keep quiet and sober so they didn't talk about the strike. Next they would sack the ore and carry it out on their backs down the hill to a safe place. When they had enough, they would hire a wagon and haul the ore to the train siding in Florissant. Harnan told them the ore would then go to Pueblo to be processed, and they would bank the cash. That way maybe they would have enough money to fight off the claims and suits when news of the strike came out.

The three made the pledge of secrecy and went back to work. They designed harnesses to use to carry the heavy ore sacks down the mountain to their cart which took it on to a wagon. Often the foot trail went past Old Man Stratton's shack on his Independence claim.

On his third trip down the hill one night, Jimmie Burns stumbled and fell, and the harness was so tight and confining that he couldn't get free of it and he couldn't stand up. Burns began to exercise his Irish prerogative and showed off his skill in swearing. Soon Stratton heard him, came out of his shack, and found Burns in the darkness. He helped Burns out of the harness and invited him into his shack for a drink.

One whiskey led to another, and before long Jimmie Burns told his longtime friend what had happened at their little splinter of a mine. He told Stratton that they had $70,000 in the bank, but they weren't sure that would be enough to fight off lawsuits.

Stratton agreed and the two pondered the problem over another drink. Before long, Stratton told Jimmie Burns about the still secret wealth of his Independence. If he could tie in with the Portland and fight off the surrounding claims, he and the Irishmen could buy up most of Battle Mountain and protect their interests and guarantee that they would become millionaires.

The two talked with the other two Irish partners at the Portland the next morning, and they quickly agreed to the plan. They worked out ways to increase the production at the Portland, and Stratton said he'd start working shifts around the clock at the Independence.

The Portland could hire men to help them, and they could haul the ore out at night in wagons until they were spotted. When the news leaked out about the Portland strike and the lawsuits were filed, they would have more cash. Between the two of them they should have enough assets to fight off all the lawyers in Colorado.

It was the middle of August when the four men shook hands and decided to work together. No contracts were drawn; it was a gentlemen's operating agreement.

The Portland put on a crew of men and swore them to silence about where they worked and how much gold ore they mined. The ore went out at night in wagons. Every day meant that much more of a nest egg to fight off the expected lawsuits.

The Independence went on a round-the-clock schedule; ore poured out and money flowed in. It wasn't until October of 1893 that the secret of the Portland bonanza leaked out.

At once lawsuits were threatened, but none reached court until the middle of November. By then both the Irishmen and their backer, Stratton, had more money in the bank. The Portland owners had $125,000 in their defense fund, and Stratton matched that amount. Stratton also had a no-limit line of credit at Irving Howbert's First National Bank of Colorado Springs.

The battle lines were drawn.

In the next few weeks, twenty-seven firms filed suit against Burns, Harnan, and Doyle. They claimed rights to the Portland vein since it did not come to the surface on the Portland claim. No one knew where it did surface, and the litigants argued that the vein might come to surface on their property and they had a right to find out. The Portland had no rights to the vein by right of the law of apex, the lawyers pleaded in their written charges.

The lawsuits claimed damages that totaled more than $3 million. Stratton had hired a lawyer to handle the lawsuits. He didn't want a local man or a slick Denver shyster who might win the day for the Portland and then cheat them all out of the mine. He hired a man from the Springs he had known for some time who he considered able, swift, and bright enough to get the job done. His name was Verner Z. Reed. The lawyer moved into the Palace Hotel in Cripple Creek and went to work.

Reed came into the highly charged contest at a furious pace. His first move was to option the Portland claim to Walter Crosby for $250,000 with an agreement that the option would never be picked up. Now the twenty-seven litigants weren't sure just who they should be suing. More precious time was gained.

Reed worked quietly, contacting the smaller claimants and settling with them, buying their claims at a fraction of their asking price. He challenged the larger and richer opponents with the threat that he would countersue them on the grounds that his new claim held prior rights to their prospect holes. There were no operating mines among the litigants.

Those who had sued this small outfit suddenly felt threatened and began to waver.

When the suits had been transferred to Walter Crosby and the cases came to court, Crosby surrendered the option back to the Irishmen, leaving the cases moot and without any standing.

As soon as the assets were back in the partners' hands, lawyer Reed dissolved the partnership and set up the Portland Gold Mining Company. He sold stock at one dollar a share and at once declared a dividend of $90,000.

The Portland stock price went through the roof, and within a few weeks the small, forgotten splinter of land on Battle Mountain, no more than 1/15th of an acre, had turned into one of Cripple Creek's richest enterprises.

Those who were preparing to sue the new company now faced a far larger and more powerful foe than the small three-man splinter company that had struck a lucky vein. Their lawyers counseled them, and most called on Reed and established bargaining sessions.

When the last litigant was satisfied, all claims of the original twenty-seven suits had been sold to the Portland Gold Mining Company. Now the partners did not own 1/15th of an acre and a vein of gold that did not apex on their land. Now they owned 183 acres and twenty-eight claims.

Buying out those who brought suit cost the Portland $1,025,000. Most of that amount had been borrowed from the bank in the Springs by Stratton.

Lawyer Reed issued three million shares at a par value of one dollar of Portland Gold Mining Company stock. Stratton was awarded 731,000 shares for his part in the contest. Doyle, Harnan, and Burns each took 600,000 shares. Most of the rest of the shares went to Frank Peck, a Springs cigar merchant, and to J.R. McKinnie, who owned the nearby gold ore producing Black Diamond mine. McKinnie traded the Black Diamond to Portland for his stock.

Winfield Scott Stratton was named president of the corporation at the first stockholders meeting, which he did not attend. He resigned and said the three Irishmen had found and developed the mine, so they should manage it. The new president was Jimmie Burns.

The Portland Gold Mining Company was the mine set at the highest altitude of any in the Cripple Creek Bonanza. It was located at 10,240 feet elevation. It also eventually was the deepest working mine with shafts down 3,200 feet.

The Portland is the all-time record holder for gold production in the Cripple Creek Mining District at $60 million. That's when gold was worth $20.67 an ounce and after 1934, $35 per ounce. Compare that to about $400 an ounce for gold today. Say the average price of Portland gold was $22 an ounce back then. That would be 2,727,272 ounces mined. At today's price that would bring in more than a billion dollars: $1,090,908,800. Not bad for a splinter mine.

In May of 1900 a corporate report was made on the Portland Gold Mining Company. It is as follows:

The Portland Gold Mining Company. Incorporated in 1894. James F. Burns, President. Irving Howbert, Vice President. Frank G. Peck, Secretary and Treasurer. Charles J. Moore, Consulting Engineer. A.T. Gunnell, General Counsel. Board Members: W. S. Stratton and John Harnan.

Main office, First National Bank block, Colorado Springs, Colorado.

3,000,000 shares. Par Value, $1.00. In treasury January 1, 1900, $602,672.10.

Owns (the following claims) The Portland, Bobtail No. 2, Doubtful, Anna Lee, White House, Hidden Treasure, Vanadium, Captain, Queen of the Hills, Scranton, Baby Ruth, National Belle, Bobtail No. 3, Four Queens, King Solomon Placer, Success, Fair Play, Cyclone, Lowell, Rosario, Black Diamond, Tidal Wave, Lost Anna, Milton, Little Harry, Devil's Own and a one-fourth interest in the Blue Stocking. In all about 183 acres, situated in section twenty-nine on Battle Mountain.

In April, 1900 the company also purchased 52.5 percent of the Total Wreck, which property is shown in the center of the plat on the opposite page. All the above property is covered by United States patent, excepting the Fair Play claim, containing about one-twentieth of an acre which is held by location.

The surface improvement and machinery consist of a dwelling house for officers of the company, dwelling house for the general manager, mine office, surveyor's office with fire-proof vault; assay office, sixty-ton railroad scale and ten-ton wagon scale; also the following shaft houses: The Burns, the Bobtail No. 2, the Scranton, and the Lowell.

One pump station on the King Solomon placer with a pump of 300 gallons capacity, boiler, and a 55,000 and two 60,000 gallon reservoirs used for fire purposes as well. The main working shaft house on the Burns is 40 x 130 feet, with a wing for boiler, 30 x 75 feet, also drying room, 11 x 30 feet, with wing for dynamo and carpenter shop. Large blacksmith shop with five forges.

A 600 horse power hoisting engine, which is the largest in the camp. The Burns shaft is a three-compartment shaft and the cages are double deckers. There is an immense compressor plant for supplying drills. Three compressors, one driving 16 drills, and one driving 24 drills. Four boilers. There are also two underground hoists, three large pumps; one of 800 gallons capacity at a depth of 900 feet; one of 1,000 gallon capacity at 1,000 feet; one of 1,200 gallons capacity at 1,000 feet lift.

The principal development work has been done on the old portion of the Anna Lee and Doubtful claims. Shaft No. 2 is now being sunk on the Captain lode, and No.3 on the Buckeye. The Portland Gold Mining

Company stands alone in the fact that none of its treasury stock has ever been offered for sale; it has all been used in the purchase of new property. All litigation has now been practically settled and the mine stands as the largest producer in the district.

The total production of ore from April 1, 1894 to January 1, 1900 is 148,139.96 tons, of a value of $8,378,732.88. The amount paid in dividends from the commencement until January 1, 1900, $2,557,080.00. A regular dividend was paid in January, 1900 consisting of 2 cents per share and 1 cent extra, amounting to $90,000.00. The last regular dividend up to the time this Manual went to press was paid April 15, 1900, $60,000. Total dividends to April 15, 1900 $2,557,080.00.

The lowest price on record for Portland stock is 26 and a half cents; the highest price for stock during 1899, $2.60 per share; lowest price for stock during 1899, $1.45 & 7/8ths per share. Price of stock May 19, 1900, $3.00.

While the lawyer in-fighting went on at the Portland to settle the claims, Stratton had been hard at work himself. He hired a lawyer to buy up with no fanfare eleven claims on Battle Mountain near his Independence, Professor Lamb, and Washington claims.

Remember, a hard rock claim was only 1,500 feet long and 300 feet wide, a little over 10.3 acres. Before summer of 1894 Winfield Scott Stratton had bought eleven claims on Battle Mountain to bring his total to fourteen that covered 112 acres. Both Stratton and the Irish trio had won the day.

As the two working gold mines hired more men and bought more equipment and shipped out more ore, the result was the speeding up of activity at the other working mines. Hagerman at his Isabella mine worked more men in his drifts and tunnels. Dave Moffat at the Victor mine put on another shift of miners and increased his production. Irving Howbert, who owned the Anchoria-Leland, increased his production of gold to keep pace with the leaders.

It was a heady time for the gold mine owners. Things were moving along fine. Halfway through the year of 1894 the population of Cripple Creek had soared to 10,000 people and the good times were rolling. None of it mattered to Bob Womack. He was in the Springs learning how to run a boarding house and not at all concerned with the tremendous economic giant that he had created just three years before.

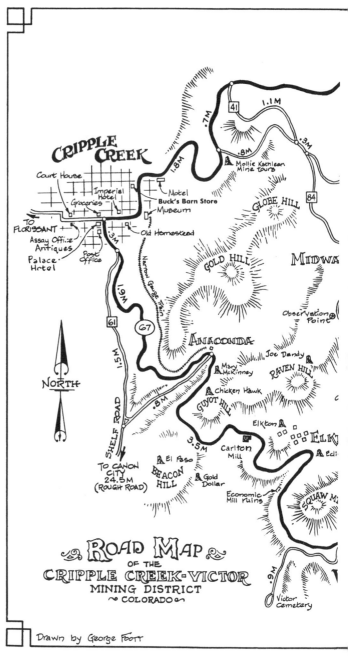

GOLD FOUND HERE. This George Foott road map drawing of the Cripple Creek and Victor Mining area shows where the mines, towns, and mountains were.

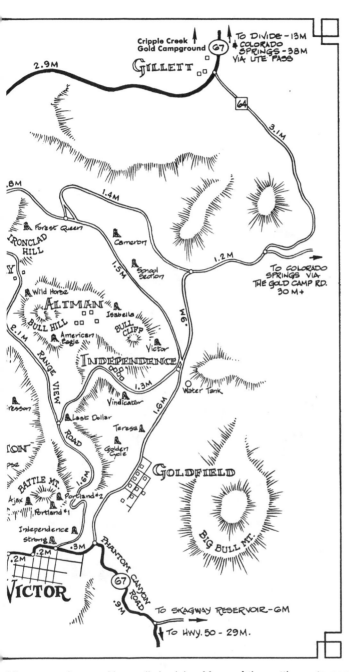

Mines are shown with small derricks. Many of the settlements named are no longer there. Take a drive! (Drawing Courtesy of George Foott, Denver, CO.)

EARLY SHAFT HOUSE of the C.O.D. mine on June 22, 1893. The man at the far right near the white horse is Spencer Penrose, a man of some importance in Cripple Creek. Could the name of the mine have been because it was started on borrowed money? (Photo Courtesy Pikes Peak Library District)

C.O.D. SHAFT HOUSE INTERIOR. The hoist engineer, one of the most important men at a deep mine, is at the far right. He's Jim Leonard. Spencer Penrose in the suit and hat is at the far left of this picture taken on May 22, 1894. (Photo Courtesy Colorado Springs Pioneer Museum)

CHAPTER 8

Red Lights: Naughty Girls

Blanche Barton stormed into Cripple Creek as the first soiled dove in town back in 1891. She plied her trade in her red striped tent near Bob Womack's shack on the slope of Poverty Gulch where she wouldn't be washed down in a flash flood.

Soon other shady ladies came to the mining camp, and the more it grew the more the influx of the fallen women to serve the men in the camp.

During the growing pains days of 1891 and 1892, the shops and stores concentrated on Myers Avenue. This included the parlour houses and brothels, mostly above the saloons such as the Buckhorn and the Anaconda.

The ladies of the evening worked both upstairs and downstairs looking for customers. The women from the houses run by madams such as Blanche Barton, Mollie King, and Minnie Smith enticed customers in the saloons and shops along Bennett Avenue.

Toward the end of 1892 the competition between the girls to get customers increased so much that it was almost impossible for a man to go into a shop or a saloon on Bennett without being propositioned a dozen times.

Most town women wouldn't go to the area to shop, and the citizens of the town figured it was time to do something about it. No city ordinance was passed, and no official action taken, but Hi Wilson, the city marshal, began moving the dance halls, the painted women, and the madams and their flocks off Bennett Avenue. He shuttled them a block south to Myers Avenue between Third and Fifth streets.

The marshal told the women that they would not be hassled by the law or the city if they stayed in that area. He told them as well that they must continue to pay their head tax to the city and donate to the churches and be on their best and quietest behavior when they went shopping.

The move worked, but it also turned Myers Avenue into one of the wildest and largest red light districts of any town in the West. Many of the town's gambling houses and saloons gravitated to Myers Avenue as well to keep the pleasures of the flesh in one concentrated "shopping" zone.

One addition to the usual brothels in Cripple Creek was the parlour houses. Some of these were elaborate affairs, finely furnished. The most famous of them was the Old Homestead. The first building that housed the brothel burned in the big fire of 1896 and was replaced by a two-story brick building.

Even the first building had electric lights, running water, a telephone, and a system of inner communications. The small, elegant bedrooms were heated with coal stoves.

Some of the best parties in the district took place in the Old Homestead's ground floor parlor and entertainment room. These were lavishly furnished with the best draperies, furniture, and decorations of the day, with a fine carpet on the floor.

One unique feature of the Old Homestead was a second-floor hallway window where a man could view the ladies available and pick out his choice for the evening. The Old Homestead not only furnished the ladies, but also served fine food and the best in wines, liquors, and entertainment. It was all done in a rich setting of red velvet, fine China, crystal chandeliers, and beautiful furniture. It was a complete package the likes of which had seldom been seen before.

For the most part, this was not a drop-in type of operation. Men made arrangements well in advance with the madam who set up firm reservations. Individual visits or parties for several men were arranged for an evening or even a weekend.

As the mines became more profitable, the newly rich mining kings used the Old Homestead to entertain out-of-town guests and business associates, often taking over the whole house for a night or weekend.

The prices were not cheap, but with such a complete package, the madams at the various parlour houses in Cripple Creek could push the prices as high as the market would bear. A few hundred dollars more on a weekend fling meant little to a gold mine owner who was worth millions.

The Old Homestead usually had five or six women "guests" in the house. To serve the customers there was also a housekeeper, two maids, two butlers, a piano player, and a porter. It was first-class all the way. Just having the cash to pay the tab many times wasn't enough at the Old Homestead. Often if the managers of the establishment didn't know a prospective client, or know of him, he wouldn't be allowed inside.

One of the most flamboyant and popular madams of the Old Homestead was Pearl De Vere. Pearl had a shadowy past—many said she came from a respectable and wealthy family somewhere in the East and that the family thought that she was designing fancy ball gowns for the wealthy women of Cripple Creek and Colorado Springs.

She often was seen riding the fanciest horse in the Welty stable called She Devil. She liked to wear a small derby hat and dark riding habit of blue with the skirt billowing out behind her. The skittish horse would prance and wheel and rear, but Pearl De Vere held her seat and controlled the animal with ease.

Now and then she would drive through the streets in a single-seated phaeton with sparkling red wheels behind a pair of high-stepping pure black horses. She might wear a taffeta dress and a wide brimmed hat in green velvet with a willow plume topping her auburn pompadour.

Sometimes she wore all brown, on other occasions a blouse with leg-o-mutton sleeves that accented her slender arms.

Suddenly rumors swept through Cripple Creek. Word came that one of Pearl De Vere's favorites had struck a rich vein in his mine and he was throwing a party to end all parties at the sumptuous Old Homestead. Plans were afoot and all sorts of special food, drink, and decorations were to be on hand.

The whole parlour house would be turned into a tropical garden with orchids, gardenias, and mimosa. French champagne shipped by the case directly from France would arrive, as well as caviar from Russia and wild turkey from Alabama for roasting.

There would be two of the best bands from Denver to play for dancing the latest schottisches, two-steps, and cakewalks. The top gossip item was that Miss De Vere had ordered a special gown from Paris that cost $800.

Accounts vary about what happened. This report from one of the Cripple Creek newspapers in June of 1897 probably strikes the middle ground.

Pearl De Vere, the mistress of the Old Homestead, died yesterday from an overdose of morphine. There is no evidence that the act was intentional, and it is the opinion of all her friends that in taking a sleeping potion, she had carelessly taken too much of the drug. The inmates of the house had been jollifying the night previous, and it was morning before they retired.

Pearl complained that her nerves were all unstrung and insisted that one of the girls should come and sleep in her room. It was eleven o'clock yesterday when the girl awoke and found Pearl lying on her face breathing heavily. She soon saw that something was wrong, and called for help. Dr. Hereford was summoned and did everything in his power, but the drug, evidently taken before going to bed, had been at work too long, and at three o'clock she died.

The body was taken to the Fairley-Lampman rooms and Coroner Marlowe sent for (from Colorado Springs). He will arrive today and hold an inquest. A deputy sheriff took possession of the house and had all the girls move out, and placed a guard over the valuables.

Pearl De Vere is well know to all the old-timers of Cripple Creek as the keeper of the Old Homestead, one of the most elegant houses of ill repute in the city.

Mabel Barbee Lee, chronicler of her remembrances of childhood days in Cripple Creek, had been enamored with the glamorous Pearl and had seen her several times on the street. After her death she wanted to see Pearl once more and as a twelve-year-old slipped into the mortuary.

From the shadows she said she saw a thin, sharp-nosed woman talking with the undertaker.

The woman was outraged. She bristled and scolded the undertaker. She said that the stain on her family would never rub off. The stain was as red as the dye on the harlot's hair. The woman insisted that the undertaker should have told her what her sister had become and the kind of life she had been leading. If she had known this she would not have made the long, futile trip to such a loathsome place. She said she would take no responsibility for the woman known as Pearl De Vere. She said she was washing her hands of such a disgraceful business.

The undertaker asked the woman if she wanted her sister buried in the potter's field.

The woman snorted and said that this harlot was no sister of hers and slammed out the door.

The high-class Eastern family had no more contact with Pearl and did not participate in her funeral.

The Elk's twenty-piece band led the march of the funeral procession for Pearl to the Mount Pisgah cemetery. Four mounted police-monitored buggies were filled with girls from "the row," and there were stacks of flowers from her admirers, some from the Springs and Denver.

Pearl was laid to rest overlooking Cripple Creek where she is remembered as the most beautiful and elegant of all of the many dozens of madams on Myers Avenue's red light district.

Other parlor houses in the district but not quite so plush as the Old Homestead on Myers Avenue included the Mikado, the Royal Inn, Neil McClusky's, and Laura Bell's. These places had a rapid turnover. Some of the others in the district at one time or another included The Place, Harem

Club, the Library, Sunnyrest, White Leaf, and the Chicken Ranch.

There were bordellos to serve every taste and purse from five- to fifteen-girl houses with no food or liquor served, to the one-girl cribs down at the end of Myers Avenue into the start of Poverty Gulch.

Often there were more than thirty of these one-girl operations staged in unpainted wooden shacks that stretched down Poverty Gulch for a quarter of a mile. Sometimes there was a separation of races in this area. Usually French girls were first down from Myers, then came the Japanese, Chinese, Mexican, and Indians, with Negroes at the far end.

Most of the pine board cribs were two-room affairs with the front room serving as the bedroom only large enough for an iron bedstead and a pair of chairs and a wood burning heating stove. In back was the girl's kitchen and private quarters.

Most of the sales work was done from the open doors or the window of the crib itself. These sales pitches were often loud and vulgar with the women showing the merchandise, to the extent they thought they needed to, to make the sale.

From time to time the authorities tried to tone down the open display and wild talk. It usually didn't work. One time the Cripple Creek city council ordered their town marshal to talk to the girls. They were told to keep their windows closed and the blinds down, their doors closed, and not to make any kind of sexual solicitation at all on the street.

The orders were given and that was the end of it. They were orders that could not be enforced and the marshal and the girls both knew it.

Directly across from the best parlour houses on Myers Avenue stood a solid block of saloons and dance halls. In the year 1900 there were seventy-three saloons in the city of Cripple Creek. Some of these in the heyday were the Last

Chance, the Terminal, Swanee River, the Abbey, Old Yellowstone, the Opera Club, the Combination, and the Dawson Club.

Also in this mix of sin and entertainment were the variety theaters. Two of the famous ones were Crapper Jack's and the Red Light. More than a dozen of these theaters were combination saloons and theaters. They all had long bars where beer sold for five cents and that included a free lunch. Most of the places also had ten-piece bands, a bevy of girls who would dance with you for a small fee, and racy burlesque shows.

The showmen in the operations weren't content to let the customers come to them. Before a performance, the band from a theater would parade up and down the avenue with their show girls in costumes and encourage the gawkers to come to their show after the parade.

Right in the middle of all of this hoopla and sin and sex stood the staid edifice of the Cripple Creek Grand Opera House. The more proper set of Cripple Creek were embarrassed and unhappy that they had to walk through the heart of sin street to reach the opera house for some wholesome, uplifting, and often educational entertainment.

The opera house was grand and would seat 1,500 patrons, by far the largest house in the area. It was considered to be a good place to perform, and all of the popular traveling companies of that day made it a point to play there.

There was lots of competition in the red light district in the last few years of the eighties and the first few of the nineties. A few over 300 women worked at the world's oldest profession in the town of about 25,000. Oversupplied is the first thought that comes to mind. However there were nearly 55,000 people in the mining district, so out of towners undoubtedly made up a lot of the customers.

The Cripple Creek treasury profited by this female work force. Each of the girls was charged a "tax" or license fee of six dollars a month. Every madam had to pay out sixteen dollars a month to do business. Remember, this was when the average working man drew down three dollars a day in the mines, and the town workers topped out at about two dollars a day.

The license permitted the girls and the madams to be employed in Cripple Creek legally, no matter what the state constitution might say. The girls were required to have a "regular" physical examination to reduce the chances of disease. There is no mention just how often "regular" meant.

The madams who provided consistently good services attained a type of blighted social standing with the men of the district and some became famous, such as Hazel Vernon, longtime madam of the Old Homestead. Some of the parties they gave were of a totally social nature that the men thoroughly enjoyed, without their wives, of course.

The girls who worked in the brothels of most types were young, many only fifteen or sixteen, and often the prettiest and best dressed women in the town. They worked at being pretty and pleasing to the men. The madams ruled these chattels with a firmness that bordered on cruelty.

As long as a girl did her work, was popular, remained in good health, and didn't get pregnant, she was protected by her house and well cared for. Usually the girls lived in the house and their needs were taken care of by the madam. They received some pay, but not much, and could use the money for what they wanted, which often turned out to be fancy clothes and to enjoy some of the luxuries that Cripple Creek housewives could only dream about.

Now and then a girl would be whisked away by an amorous miner or mine owner and married. It was a dream of many of the soiled doves in the nesting houses of Cripple Creek, but a dream that seldom came true.

Most houses had from five to fifteen girls. When they lost their appeal in the highest priced houses, and they wanted to stay in town, they would move "down a step" to a lower pay scale house and go to work again. At the bottom of the heap were the "freelance" women who were almost all older and less attractive than the house girls. These were the ones who worked out of individual cribs along the far end of Myers Avenue and well into Poverty Gulch.

The cribs had no numbers, and usually the only indication of who lived there was a name scrawled on the door. The name would be the colorful nickname of the lady involved and served for identification and advertising as well. Life for these girls was tough.

Away from the houses on shopping trips to the stores, the ladies of the evening looked like any other well-dressed woman in the district. Store owners said they were good customers, quiet and polite, and usually had money to pay for what they wanted. Sometimes credit would be extended, and if there was any problem with collecting, the merchants always knew they could get their investment back by taking the cost out in trade at the parlour house.

After the night was over, and before the "show" was to go on the next day, many of these young women were tormented alcoholics or drug addicts and lived lonely and often tragic lives.

A story from a newspaper from Cripple Creek in early 1900:

Blanch Garland of the Bon Ton Dance Hall died at 2:00 this morning from taking two ounces of chloroform. A quarrel with her lover was the cause of the deed.

Another story from an early district paper:

> Lucile Morris, for some time an inmate of the
> Mikado (a parlour house), attempted to take her life
> by taking a dose of carbolic acid and is now between
> life and death at Sister's Hospital.

A news story from a 1903 newspaper:

> Nellie Rolfe, a woman of the half world, was found
> dead in her room at 377 Myers avenue at about 4
> o'clock yesterday afternoon by a woman living near
> the home of the deceased. The cause of death is not
> known, and whether or not the woman committed
> suicide is a question.
>
> When found the woman was in a crouched position
> on the floor leaning against the bed with her head
> resting on her arm. She had in all probability been
> dead for several hours, as the muscles were tightly
> drawn.
>
> The woman was a victim to the morphine habit.
> Three small bottles of the drug and two hypodermic
> syringes were found on the dresser of her room.

Not only were drugs, alcohol, and suicide common with
the "lost angels," but sickness as well. The ten-thousand-
foot altitude of Cripple Creek and the cold winter nights
often resulted in pneumonia. The sickness was dreaded by
everyone in that day since there was no known cure and
recovery was something of a small miracle despite the best
efforts of the early physicians.

Dangerous and addictive drugs in that time were not illegal. Heroin, morphine, and opium were easy to buy from
the local drug stores. The young boys hawking newspapers
and messenger boys were usually the runners. A girl in a
house or crib would give him a special playing card that had
a meaning between her and the pharmacist.

The dance hall girls were a breed apart. Some of them had been whores in time past, but now they were not pretty enough or clever enough to hold down a spot in a good parlour house. They would hire out to the dance halls where they were "taxi" dancers, charging for each dance. Many of the girls used the dance hall as a hunting ground for one or two or three beddings a night with the dancers.

They were usually less pretty, sweet, and talented, but they were considered a step up from the girls in the one-room cribs down on Poverty Gulch row.

One Myers Avenue legend is that a crib girl called Leo the Lion made her way to Fourth and Myers Avenue in the heart of the red light district exactly at noon one day and took off all her clothes. She stood there naked and began shouting at the top of her voice.

"I'm Leo the Lion, the queen of the row." After proclaiming her queenship several times, she let some miners who knew her take her back to her crib to sleep off her alcoholic demonstration.

In 1915 the saga of Myers Avenue ended. The city council officially changed the name to Julian Street after the man who had written an unflattering article about Cripple Creek, concentrating on Myers Avenue. The cribs and parlour houses were empty and deserted. Most of the saloons and variety theaters were closed. The wild days of Myers Avenue had come to an end.

THE SOILED DOVES WORKED Bennett Avenue for a while, but when they became too sales oriented, the city fathers moved them back to Myers Avenue a block over. Then the ladies of Cripple Creek could shop on Bennett Avenue without being offended. This Bennett Avenue picture is before the fire, probably 1894. It also is before the Midland Terminal Depot was built at the end of the street. (Photo Courtesy Colorado Springs Pioneer Museum)

CHAPTER 9

Cripple's First Millionaire

Winfield Scott Stratton has been called the second most important man in the Cripple Creek Bonanza. If Bob Womack hadn't found that first gold vein on the El Paso claim, Cripple Creek might not have been discovered for twenty years more or perhaps not at all.

Then came Winfield Scott Stratton to work his magic on the claims and mines of Cripple Creek and become the first of over thirty millionaires produced by the gold in the Cripple Creek District.

Stratton was born in Kentucky the year the California forty-niners charged to the golden state and the Sutter's Mill gold rush. His birthplace was not far from where Bob Womack began life. His father was a carpenter, a shipbuilder, and he taught his son the trade. Stratton was the only boy in a ten-sister family, and he soon left home to find his fortune.

WINFIELD SCOTT STRATTON, later in life. He was Cripple Creek's first millionaire, but he never put on airs. He always thought of himself as a working man. He poured $8 million back into Cripple Creek on a scheme that never produced a dollar's worth of gold. (Photo Courtesy Colorado Springs Pioneer Museum)

He wandered to Iowa, then to Omaha, Nebraska, and on to Lincoln. In 1872, when he was twenty-three years old, he moved to Colorado Springs and set up a carpenter business. He was good at it, talented and inventive. Soon he had all the work he wanted. In the next two years he set up three different business partnerships that ended in disputes.

He was a fine carpenter but not a diplomat and had little use for people. His growing up in a house with eleven women gave him a great desire never to have anything to do with them. By 1874 he was tired and fed up with carpentry. He had heard about the silver mining in the San Juan mountains in southwestern Colorado. He invested his savings, $2,800, a lot of money in those days, in a mining claim called the Yretaba Silver Lode and went south to become a millionaire.

He didn't. He put in two months on the claim learning all he could about mining and silver and quickly found out that he had thrown away his money on a worthless venture. The sum of $2,800 was three years' wages for a working man.

However, he had been fascinated with his prospecting and mining experience. He felt that this was the life he wanted to lead, searching for precious metals. There was excitement, thrills of discovery, and not a lot of people to deal with who told him one thing and changed their mind when he had the job half over or the project built.

He would be a prospector. He reveled in the high country, the water splashing down a hillside, the remote wonder of it all. Life was basic and simple. He could rely on his only traveling companion, a burro that never talked back to him or complained or yelled or argued.

Stratton knew that he had to earn a living. Although he didn't have much formal education, he was sharp, good with figures, intelligent, ambitious, and inquisitive. He went back to Colorado Springs and continued his carpentry work. All winter he slaved at his trade, earning enough for a new grub stake as soon as spring broke.

Then he was off prospecting again. During seventeen years of this he covered a lot of ground. He worked the Chalk Creek area near Mount Princeton. He went back to the San Juans and scratched and dug his way through

Baker's Park. Then he rushed to Leadville in the early times of the big silver strike.

Later he prospected Red Cliff and Aspen, Kokomo, Robinson, even Rosita in the wet Mountain Valley and Elk Mountain. He found nothing.

Stratton realized the more he knew about ore and mining, the better chance he would have of finding something worthwhile. He spent one summer employed at the Nashold reduction mill at Brekenridge to learn more about ore. At one point he took the course in blowpipe analysis from Professor Lamb at Colorado College. Later he studied metallurgy at the Colorado School of Mines in Golden.

He was on another of his summer forays into the mountains when he showed up in Cripple Creek in May of 1891. By this time Stratton was no longer a pup. He had passed his forty-second birthday. His hair had turned from brown to silky white, and he was pale and thin. His generous moustache also showed as a white swatch across his face.

He liked Bob Womack but had little faith in his prospecting ability or his choice of a claim. He moved to what he considered to be the south lip of the ancient cauldron and set out his claim stakes for the Washington, the Professor Lamb, and the Independence.

He had little luck with any of them, and in June he went back to the Springs only to learn that that the building industry there had hit rock bottom. With no prospects there, he returned to his shack above Wilson Creek and his claims. When he arrived, he found a man waiting for him who wanted to buy the Washington claim.

Stratton asked him why he wanted to buy the claim.

The man's name was L.M. Pearlman, and he represented mining interests in San Francisco. His firm thought that the Washington claim was a marginal bet at best, but they were set up to take a gamble now and then.

Stratton must have figured that the big money liked the Washington claim because it was near the Strong mine which had been producing ore now for some months.

Pearlman kept downgrading the chances that the Washington would ever produce, and that irritated Stratton. At first he had been delighted at the chance to unload the Washington. Only a few months before he had offered it to several money men in the Springs for $500 but found no takers.

He decided not to sell the Washington but another claim. He figured quickly and made impossible terms.

He told Pearlman he could have the Independence claim instead of the Washington on a thirty-day option. Total price: $155,000, with $5,000 down and the balance on picking up the option at the end of the thirty days.

Stratton had quoted a price that was outlandish for an unproved claim that had produced no gold ore. It was priced twice as high as what Count Pourtales paid for the Buena Vista.

The buyer wrote out a check for $5,000 closing the deal and taking the thirty-day option to buy and take possession.

Stratton had a chance to make $155,000 from the unproductive Independence. In 1893 that was a fortune, more than most working men could make in a lifetime. A miner's $3-a-day wage brought a yearly income of $1,000 a year if he didn't get hurt or killed.

Pearlman told Stratton that his men would take over the mine the first thing in the morning. If there were any tools or equipment he wanted to claim, he should get it all out of there that day.

Stratton went to the shaft on the Independence and started down the eighty-five-foot hole. There were four working crosscuts at the fifty-foot level. He removed his shovels, drills, hammers, and other tools from three of the crosscuts where he had been digging.

The fourth cross drift had been abandoned the year before as he looked in other areas for a vein of gold. He almost passed it by, but decided there could be some shovels or picks or old drills in there. The entrance was half closed by a rock fall. He dug out part of it and worked his way in with a lantern. He found one shovel worth saving and an old drill. On his way out of the crosscut he poked at the wall with the drill.

The drift looked no better now than it had a year ago. As he walked along he jabbed the iron drill into the wall again several times. Small rocks fell down here and there. Then at one point several rocks fell at his feet and he shifted the lantern up to see where they had come from.

He must have stared in amazement at the discolored rocks on the side of the drift. They were what he had been searching for. They were the outer edge of a vein of ore. Stratton kept poking with the drill, went for a pick and hammer, and cut out more of the edge of the vein. He worked for two more hours, tracking the vein down the tunnel for twenty-seven feet. After another hour Stratton knew he had found a gloriously thick vein of rich ore. He took out various ore samples from across the vein as far as he could reach. There was one small problem. He had just signed a thirty-day option to sell the Independence.

He didn't own it any more, at least not for thirty days.

Stratton pondered his situation. Nothing in his agreement with Pearlman said he had to tell the man about his new find. Cautiously he replaced the rock he had removed to get into the crosscut. He pushed back an old timber and made the crosscut look exactly the way it had when he came down the shaft. When finished it looked as it had before, an abandoned tunnel that had been given up on a year ago.

He took out all of his tools and equipment and moved them to the Washington claim. Then he picked up his bag of ore samples and went across the ridge to Squaw Gulch and showed them to the assayer, N. B. Guyot, who had an assay furnace.

Guyot, who had been producing unhappy assays for Stratton for months, must have smiled when he read off the figures this time.

The assay showed that the ore samples would produce $380 a ton. He didn't ask from what claim it came. He would do his best to forget the assay. Men in his trade had to have close mouths and short memories or they didn't last long.

On the way home, Stratton was elated. The vein had to be at least nine feet thick. Even at a gentle taper it had to extend downward for a hundred feet. That meant there could be $3 million worth of ore in sight!

Back at his cabin, Stratton pondered his situation. Pearlman owned rights to the Independence for thirty days. He had the option of paying an inflated $150,000 price tag at the end of that time to buy the mine outright. The odds were that Pearlman and his workers would not find anything in the Independence, since Stratton had not found a thing in two years of work. If so, he should get the Independence back when Pearlman and company refused to pick up the option and the mine at the end of the thirty days.

The next day he went to his Washington mine, sweating for six hours in a tunnel to work off some of his frustration. July 1893 was the longest month ever known to humankind.

Pearlman's option expired on July 28. Stratton could see the six-man crew working in the Independence. He steeled himself to stay away from the claim. He had to be totally indifferent to what happened over there.

Stratton admitted later that he had wild, terrifying dreams about Pearlman's crew going into the fourth tunnel and finding his bonanza. More than once he awoke in a sweat and fought down the nightmare.

Day after day, Stratton worked other claims, talked with other miners, anything to avoid thinking about the Independence.

At last the month had almost expired. Stratton talked to Pearlman and arranged to take him to dinner on July 27, the night before the option ended.

Pearlman was glum.

Stratton took him to the Palace Hotel, on the corner of Bennett Avenue and Second Street. It had the best dining room in town. It was the meeting place for the important and rich and famous of Cripple Creek. It had a big lobby, and a fire burned in the large fireplace on winter days and on chill summer evenings.

After the meal, the two miners pulled up chairs in front of the fire and talked about the mine.

Pearlman was frank. He told Stratton that his crew hadn't found anything remarkable. He said they hadn't found enough gold ore to cover the cost of the option, let alone the expenses of the crew.

The men lit cigars and sipped at after-dinner brandies as they watched the flames dance on the pine logs in the fireplace.

Pearlman told Stratton that his crew had worked the three main crosscuts where he had been digging. They found nothing worthwhile.

Stratton's hopes must have been rising. Then Pearlman reported that the fourth drift didn't look productive so they had left it to last.

The fire crackled. Stratton must have begun to sweat.

Pearlman said he had previously planned on putting his crew in the fourth drift tomorrow on the last day on a whim. Then he said he hated to waste that much more money on wages on a dry hole.

Pearlman told Stratton that he wanted to leave the first thing in the morning. He asked if Stratton would take back the option tonight and they would be finished with it.

Stratton recovered quickly from the surprise and nodded his acceptance. Pearlman took the option paper from his pocket and held it out to Stratton. Stratton later said he didn't want to risk putting out his hand because it was trembling so.

Stratton gave a short laugh and waved at the fireplace. He told Pearlman to toss the option agreement into the fire.

Pearlman nodded and pitched the folded paper into the fire. The two men watched it burn, then Pearlman offered his hand and went up to his room.

Stratton must have had a moment of total joy. He owned the Independence again!

It took him two days to round up a crew of the eight men he wanted. He put them to work in the fourth crosscut. Within two weeks he had sixteen men at work.

In quick order he designed the surface buildings he wanted and contracted to have them built. He arranged to ship his ore down the mountain to Florissant and on to Pueblo. Within a month he should be in full production. He estimated he would be taking out thirty tons of high-grade ore a day. That should round off to about $2,000 in gold at the smelter.

Calmly he decided to limit his production to that. No sense in taking out more gold ore than he needed. He liked the security, the understanding that he had at least $3 million in gold in his mountain.

It was the end of the long series of defeats and troubles of Winfield Scott Stratton. After seventeen years of prospecting he had stumbled on his bonanza by accident and then almost lost it.

He didn't limit his mining to the $2,000 a day. By the end of six months he had taken out enough ore that he had produced a million dollars in gold. That was $5,500 a day. He must have looked back and smiled at his winter carpenter chores when he was pleased to make three dollars a day.

IN THE PALACE HOTEL Stratton had his 30-day option returned on the gold rich Independence mine. He almost lost it and sweated out a 30-day option with the right to buy. The Palace Hotel was where the important people in town met to make deals. The stage also stopped out front. (Photo Courtesy Pikes Peak Library District)

THE ENGINEERS' ROOM AT THE INDEPENDENCE in 1893. These cables and controls lifted the shaft cars holding men and ore and were the heart of the deep mines. Here Winfield Scott Stratton, owner of the mine, takes a turn at the controls. (Photo Courtesy Colorado Springs Pioneer Museum)

CHAPTER 10

Other Towns in the District

As new mines developed throughout the district, small settlements sprung up to be near the mines and to serve them. There were at least seven of these smaller communities in the Cripple Creek Mining District besides the town of Cripple Creek.

The largest of these was Victor. It was about six miles from Cripple Creek on the southern rim of the great cauldron and south of Battle Mountain and Squaw Mountain near the Independence, the Strong, and the Portland mines. The town, which included settlements of Hollywood, Lawrence, Portland Station, and Strong's Camp, was platted November 6, 1893, and at the peak of its development had about 12,000 people.

The Woods Investment Company promoted the town of Victor in 1893 and placed it on the Mt. Rosa placer property on the south slope of Battle Mountain.

It began with a group of white tents and a few log cabins. A year later the Woods company struck a vein of ore while excavating for the Victor hotel. It became the Gold Coin mine in the heart of the town and proved to be the mainstay of the small community by producing gold ore for many years.

With four or five large mines right in its backyard, Victor grew quickly and soon reached its peak of population. It had two railroads servicing it and its mines, a $30,000 opera house which could seat 1,200 patrons, a new city hall and jail, and a reliable water system.

Victor was rich, fat, and satisfied. Then on August 21, 1899, fire broke out in a small saloon, and before it could be controlled the heart of Victor was leveled as the pine board buildings went up like a large bonfire. Fourteen square blocks of the city had been leveled into piles of ashes and blackened timbers. Some figured the damage at $2 million.

At once the people of Victor began to rebuild their town. This time it was made of stone and what they called "pressed bricks." This time Victor would not burn down.

Victor had become a magnet for the area's bad boys. Two rival criminal gangs holed up in Victor and knew well the tunnels in the mines under the town to use as hideouts.

One of the gangs was run by Jack Smith. He had such ex-convicts as Jack McMahon and Ed Riley on his team and soon recruited Shorty McLain, who blew up the Strong mine in 1894 during the labor strike.

Another notorious gang in Victor in those times was the Crumley group. It was led by Newt, Grant, and Sherman Crumley. Some said they had been members of the Dalton gang and escaped the famous showdown at Coffeyville, Kansas, back in 1892.

Sherman was the boss, and his brother Grant ran saloons in Cripple Creek. For a while they held up trains, robbing the passengers. Then they concentrated on stealing mine equipment and selling it back to the mine owners.

High grading became profitable and the Crumleys went into it big time, hiring men to hide high grade ore in mines, and then sending in men at night to get the ore and bring it out where it would be sold to assayers who extracted the gold and wouldn't ask questions.

The practice of high grading boomed for a while. Miners could chip off rich ore from a vein and hide it in shoe tops or in pockets or secret bags sewn in their clothes. Rich gold ore could often return to the thief as much as twenty dollars a pound. This was a big incentive to miners who worked all day for three dollars.

The night riders were men who went into the mines to pick up hidden caches of gold ore that their accomplices had chipped out of veins and hidden in drifts or on top of timbers while working. Then they split the profits.

Guards had orders to shoot to kill anyone found in a closed mine and especially at night on one-shift operations. Many a night rider got lost in a mine and wasn't found until the next morning. Sometimes the night rider would not know the shafts and tunnels well enough and fall down an open shaft to his death.

High grading was a continuing problem for all mines, especially those with rich veins. At some of the mines changing rooms were set up where every miner had to change clothes before he left the mine. Theoretically this would prevent the men from carting out high grade ore in their pants or their pockets.

Anaconda was another of the small towns that sprung up to keep miners close to the mines they worked. Anaconda was south of Gold Hill near the Mary McKinney mine and north of Guyot Hill.

The gulch below the mine is where Anaconda sprang up. The little town was platted in 1894 and at its peak held a thousand souls.

The *Cripple Creek Morning Times* reported on January 1, 1899:

The activity of Anaconda and the crowded condition of the switches, attest the fullness of the city's claim of being the chief producer of the district. Her warrants are at par. Her people are out of debt. The class of homes is of the best—nice cottages dotting the hills on either side of the stream.

Anaconda was a consolidation of the areas known as Mound City, Squaw Gulch, and Barry. Today there is nothing left of the small town except the jail.

Goldfield was the third largest town in the district during its heyday. It was founded on January 8, 1895, and is located on the south rim of the huge cauldron to the west of Big Bull Mountain. In the boom years it held as many as 3,500 people. Many of the men worked at one of the mines close by such as the Golden Cycle, the Vindicator, the Teresa, the Portland, and the Independence.

Goldfield was only a mile or so north of Victor. Because it had a fairly level area around it, Goldfield was picked for the freight and switching yards for both the Florence & Cripple Creek railroads and the later arriving Midland Terminal line.

The Goldfield streets were laid out in a careful gridwork, and the town was said to have the most sidewalks in the district. The townsite itself was entirely covered by surface locations of mining claims. Goldfield was said to have neat and comfortable residences with well-kept lawns.

North of Goldfield and just beyond the Vindicator mine about halfway around the side of the giant cauldron, stood the small town of Independence. It came into existence on November 12, 1894, and by 1900 had 1,500 people. This included the settlement called the Hull City Placer.

The town of Altman was platted on September 25, 1893, and in the good times around 1900 boasted nearly 1,500 residents. Altman stood almost on the top of Bull Hill in the low saddle between it and Bull Cliff. At 10,620 feet it was said to be the highest incorporated town in the whole country.

Sam Altman planned the town. It was close to three of the big mines, the Buena Vista, the Victor, and the Pharmacist. In Victor was where John Calderwood organized the miners into the district's first union, a local affiliated with the Western Federation of Miners.

Altman played a big part in the union strike of 1894 and the battle of Bull Hill. For a while after 1896, Altman flourished with a main street and a hotel and restaurants and saloons. Most of the men worked in the mills. No water was available that high on the mountain, so they piped it in from Grassy Gulch two miles away and had to move the water upward a thousand feet. The small town did have a power plant that produced electricity for lights in homes and stores. Almost nothing of the town remains today.

Gillett is remembered as the only town in the nation up to that time to stage a traditional Spanish bullfight. Joe Wolfe held the event over protests of the humane society and local animal rights people and lots of politicians both local and national.

A racetrack at Gillett along the Midland Terminal railroad in West Beaver Park was used. Joe built a 5,000-seat amphitheatre and advertised tickets for two to five dollars.

As it turned out, the Secretary of the Treasury refused to let Mexican bulls be imported into the States from Mexico, and Joe had to use local bulls. Over three thousand attended the first bullfight on August 24, 1895. During the fight Joe was arrested and acquitted in the Gillett Justice of Peace court the same day.

Gillett was the site of a reduction plant for processing gold ore from local mines. It could handle a hundred tons of gold ore a day and was a chlorination plant that employed a hundred men year-round.

Gillett itself didn't produce much gold ore. It was a "one-man area" where each man financed his own hole and did his own digging. There was never enough outside money invested in the mines there to make them pay off big.

Elkton was one of the small communities that grew in the district like a wild mushroom. In 1900 it had 2,500 people but was never platted as an official city. It included other small settlements called Arequa, Beacon, and Eclipse. It was near the Elkton mine midway between Raven Hill and Squaw Mountain toward the southern part of the district.

Elkton was a typical mining village where the men worked in the mines. It was on the railroad route and received some fame as the spot where Frank Lupton, a Victor policeman, beat up a Victor bully and hauled him off to jail. A friend tried to help and Lupton handcuffed the two belligerents together and then to himself and hauled them toward the Victor jail.

The two men had lots of friends, and they gathered at the Victor jail to prevent Lupton from entering. Lupton decided to transport the two men to the Cripple Creek jail on the train. The mob followed, but Lupton discouraged them by firing his six-gun into the air.

When the train pulled into Gillett around Squaw Mountain, another mob of friends had gathered. Lupton used his prisoners as a shield, but the mob pushed into Lupton's car. He fired into the gang, killing an innocent bystander. The mob faded away and Lupton put his charges into jail in Cripple Creek until it was safe to take them back to Victor.

Today only Cripple Creek and Victor remain as continuing small towns in the district. Both are skeletons of the small cities they used to be. Of the other mining villages and settlements in the district, only a few foundations and an occasional lonesome brick building remain. The land has reclaimed the towns as its own again.

Even in the boom times, most of the residents of the smaller towns and settlements went either to Victor or to Cripple Creek to do their shopping and to get supplies, or a drink or a wild night on the town. That part hasn't changed much in the Cripple Creek Mining District.

TIME TO GO TO WORK at the Orpha Mae mine on Bull Hill near the settlement of Altman. Miners worked eight hours deep underground for three dollars a day. All are wearing hats, many kinds of hats. (Photo Courtesy Pikes Peak Library District)

CHAPTER 11

Strike Time

When things are going too smoothly, you can almost count on a big fall coming. Cripple Creek had been booming, more mines opening, more big money coming in, the mines in operation producing well, and the miners taking home good pay. The owners were getting rich. They wanted it to go on forever.

In 1893 the country and the whole world was in a depression. The nation went off the silver standard and silver mines all over Colorado closed down when silver prices plummeted. Many of the miners came to Cripple Creek where the economy was growing each month. Cripple Creek probably had the most booming economy of anywhere in the United States that summer.

Wage scales differed in the mines. Some paid three dollars a day for eight hours. Some paid two dollars and fifty cents for eight hours. Some mine owners paid three dollars for nine hours.

The superintendent at the Buena Vista mine, Bradford Locke, posted a notice. It was in August of 1893, and he told

Chapter 11

the workers that they would be paid three dollars a day but would have to work nine hours instead of eight starting the next day.

The morning shift read the notice and the men gathered in a large group and didn't go to work in the tunnels. When Locke came the miners surged around him, and he tried to shout them down. One man waved a can of tar and a brush, and Locke promptly tore down his notice and left the work day at eight hours.

There was no union among the Cripple Creek miners. Up to this point there had been no need for one. Now the men began wondering about organizing.

Into this mix of various wages at different mines came John Calderwood. He had worked in the Scotland mines when he was nine years old, came to the U.S. and did time in the Pennsylvania coal field mines, and later went to the McKeesport School of Mines. Then he became involved with the Mollie Maguires, an extremist labor organization.

He came to Cripple Creek after working as a union organizer for the Western Federation of Miners in Butte, Montana. There a strike ended in the owner's favor after the U.S. Army regiments marched in and broke the strike.

Calderwood heard about the bonanza at Cripple Creek and arrived there in the fall of 1893. In two months he organized WFM unions in Altman, Cripple Creek, Victor, and Anaconda. He won over two thirds of the miners in the district and had 800 men in his union. They set their sights on an eight-hour day for three dollars a day for every man in the district.

The owners bellowed in rage. Most were fiercely independent and self-made men and hated the idea of a union. This was the biggest drawback to the mine owners coming to any kind of a united stand. After a lot of dickering, twelve of the mine owners hammered out an agreement. Starting

102

February 1, 1894, they all would operate on a nine-hour day and pay three dollars.

Owners agreeing to this rate included Jimmie Burns of the Portland, Hagermann, Dave Moffat, Irving Howbert, William Lennox, Sam Altman, and Ed De La Vergne.

When word of the united front of the twelve mines spread, Calderwood drew first blood. He called out his men from those twelve mines—500 union miners.

Workers in the mines on an eight-hour day, about 700, were not affected, and union and nonunion men kept working.

Mine owners counted their profits and figured that the miners would soon get hungry and tired of not working and go back to the tunnels. Some of these mine owners were veterans of strikes in Leadville and Aspen where the bumbling Knights of Labor led strikes that had been quickly squelched.

Calderwood surprised them. He kept control of his men. He helped persuade Jimmie Burns to keep the Portland on an eight-hour day, and he was on good social terms with both Burns and Winfield Scott Stratton of the Independence and the Washington mines, both on eight-hour days.

Calderwood quickly set up services for the strikers. In Altman, the center of the nine-hour mines, he established a central kitchen where families could get food. He talked to the strikers about what the union would do for them. He taught them what pickets and strikers could and couldn't do and stay within the law.

As the weeks crept by, the shut down mines' owners realized they had a fight on their hands.

Calderwood assessed each working union miner a $15-a-month strike fund fee and raised $4,500. He received donations from W.F.M. members in the San Juan of $700 to help. He solicited $1,400 from Cripple Creek businessmen and $800 from the union headquarters in Butte, Montana.

Most of the twelve struck mines were on Bull Hill, and by the middle of March, six weeks after the start of the strike, the owners realized that the miners were not starving and begging for their jobs back.

Public opinion generally was on the miners' side, chiding the mine owners for trying to squeeze another hour's work out of the miners, when the owners had been making money on their eight-hour shifts.

The first contract with the union was a staggering blow to the other mine owners. Winfield Stratton negotiated with Calderwood, and they agreed to a wage scale of $3.25 for a nine-hour day. Night shift workers did eight hours for the same $3.25.

Mine owners screamed and shouted at Stratton. They said it was criminal for Stratton even to talk to Calderwood, let alone to sign a contract with the hated Western Federation of Miners criminal culprits.

Another important player in the game was Colorado Governor Davis H. Waite. He was sixty-seven years old and had been elected on the splinter Populist party ticket when the Republicans and Democrats fought each other to a standstill and voted Waite as a protest.

Waite was an incompetent and described as being "not smart." Waite made wild speeches, made terrible appointments to state offices, and generally ruled with a fist of mush. The vital factor here was that he also controlled the state militia and could call them out.

The mine owners knew that he hated them, and if there was any violence in the struggle, the state militia would be called out and would support the miners, not the mine owners. This kept the owners from trying to open their mines by force.

The nine-hour group of owners got a restraining order from the court in the Springs to stop the union from interfering with the operation of their mines. Cripple Creek was still in El Paso County at that time and Colorado Springs was the county seat. On March 15 the sheriff of El Paso County, Frank Bowers, puffed up the mountain to Altman and served notice on Calderwood and a hundred members of the local union. He read off those named in the injunction and then quickly returned to Cripple Creek. He hated being caught in the middle of this strike between men he knew.

The injunction made no difference whatsoever in the strike at this point.

That same afternoon the superintendent of the Victor mine called the sheriff at Cripple Creek and told him that a mob of Altman miners was ready to wreck the Victor mine. Sheriff Bowers sent six deputies up the steep hill in a wagon to control the situation.

As soon as they arrived, the deputies were overpowered, roughed up, and taken prisoner by the Altman town officials and a group of miners who said they were the new Altman police force.

Sheriff Bowers heard of the men's capture about midnight and tried to organize a posse of Cripple Creekers to charge up the hill and free the lawmen. This posse was made up of hangers on in the saloons, and many were well into their cups.

Just before the posse left on the rescue mission, the missing deputies came straggling into town unhurt and said they were released by the Altman authorities. Sheriff Bowers sent his posse back to the saloons and to their beds.

The next morning Cripple Creek was jolted with the announcement by printed leaflets that the Victor, Anaconda, Raven, and Summit mines would open with nonunion workers. Anyone wanting to work was invited up to Bull Hill.

Everyone moving into the area would need a pass signed by Calderwood.

The sheriff feared there would be terrible violence if a hundred "scabs" tried to cross into the mines blockaded by the striking miners of Bull Hill. He wanted to call out his posse of the night before, but many of them were still sleeping off their drunks, and hangovers were the order of the day.

Sheriff Bowers must have envisioned hundreds of men wounded, beaten, or dead if the two groups of men clashed at the four mines. He worried all day, asked for advice, and at midnight, called on Governor Waite to send in the Colorado state militia.

Now the second armed force moved into the battle of Cripple Creek. The governor had troubles in Denver and he used this military emergency to take pressure off his Denver problems. He sent parts of two regiments of the Colorado state militia by train to Cripple Creek.

Commanding the troops were Colorado Adjutant General Thomas J. Tarsney and General E.J. Brooks. The troops arrived in Cripple Creek Sunday morning, March 18, 1894 and set up camp near George Carr's ranch house.

Lawyer Tarsney talked to Sheriff Bowers who told him that Calderwood, the union leader, had taken control of Bull Hill and established a reign of terror. Bowers then hurried to the Springs to get arrest warrants for Calderwood and others on the hill.

Tarsney sent word he wanted to talk to Calderwood at the Palace Hotel in Cripple Creek. He came. The adjutant general told Calderwood when Bowers came back with the warrants he would have to send the militia against the miners on the hill if they resisted arrest.

Calderwood knew that if that happened, the strike would be broken and the mine owners could send in their nonunion men and win the day. Tarsney knew that would make the governor furious because he had promised that big money interests would not dominate.

Calderwood nodded. He thought a minute, then said they would surprise the sheriff. None of them on the hill would oppose the sheriff when he came up. They would let him arrest them and take them to the Springs.

Tarsney guaranteed Calderwood that he could see that all those arrested would be acquitted of the charges in the Springs or released on five-dollar bail.

The two lifted their glasses in a toast.

Tarsney promptly rounded up his troops and marched them out of sight up Tenderfoot Hill well away from Cripple Creek.

Bowers fumed when he came back to Cripple Creek with the arrest warrants issued by the court and found the militia gone. He berated Tarsney. Bowers was sure that without any support he'd be shot to pieces going up Bull Hill.

Tarsney told him he was exaggerating. He reminded the sheriff that the militia couldn't arrest any of the strikers. He talked the lawman into going up to Altman and see if there was any resistance. If there was any gunfire, Tarsney said he would bring in the troops.

Somewhat reassured but still worried, Sheriff Bowers set out for Altman on his mare with reluctance. To his surprise, he was not shot at once. He was greeted cordially along the five-mile road by the miners, and none of them was even armed.

He made it to Altman where Calderwood met him like a visiting dignitary and poured him the best bourbon in the tiny town. To the sheriff's surprise, Calderwood and his top lieutenants surrendered meekly and were taken down the hill to Cripple Creek and then to Colorado Springs.

It was only later that Sheriff Bowers figured it out. Tarsney and Calderwood had worked together to make it look like the emergency was over on Bull Hill so Tarsney could order the troops home and not have to act in the mine owners' behalf.

The mine owners evidently saw the dangers in trying to open the mines with scabs, and with the military gone back down the tracks to Denver, they didn't have a chance to try it in March.

A few days after the arrests were made, the eighteen miners cited on Bull Hill and John Calderwood were found innocent of charges or released on a low bail.

The second armed and presumably dangerous force came toward Cripple Creek on May 25, 1894. The strike was still on. The strikers had hired a pack of lawless ex-convicts and ne'r-do-wells who terrorized some of the adjoining territory around Bull Hill, making life miserable for many.

The El Paso county officials figured they would take enforcement into their own hands and forget about help from the governor. Cripple Creek and Bull Hill were still in El Paso County, which included Colorado Springs.

Officials there hired 125 ex-police and ex-firemen fired in Denver by the governor for opposing his rule in a standoff with the militia.

Now El Paso Sheriff Bowers brought the 125 men in to help "enforce the law" and put down the strikers.

The men were armed and deputized as El Paso County deputy sheriffs. They came by rail approaching Cripple Creek from the south on the Florence & Cripple Creek railroad.

"General" Johnson, the ex-Westpoint man booted out just before graduation, led the strikers' forces. He heard about the train coming with the armed deputies.

On the morning of May 25, two flatcars carried the 125 men on the tracks toward the town of Victor. The new deputies saw nothing unusual as their train moved along close to the Strong mine on Bull Hill.

Then "General" Johnson's defensive attack came. The Strong mine's shaft house exploded with the roar of a thousand cannons. The small building blew 300 feet into the air and was smashed into kindling by the great blast.

The Denver ex-cops stared in surprise and then terror at the force of the explosion. Then before they could recover, a second blast even larger than the first one went off as the Strong mine's steam boiler blasted into the sky like a launching rocket.

The new deputies had seen enough. They ducked for cover as thousands of pieces of timbers, steel, cable, and iron showered down on the two flatcars and the train.

The train's engineer knew when to cut his losses. He pushed the train into reverse and spun his drive wheels as the train slowed, stopped, and began to move back the way it had come. Soon it was in reverse flight back down the tracks.

Johnson tried to follow up on his success. He liberated a flatcar and loaded it with dynamite and sent it rolling on the downgrade following the Denver ex-cops and short-term deputies. The flat car, with no one on board to brake, gained too much speed and flew off the tracks on a curve. The powder exploded on impact, but instead of killing the Denver hired guns, it blew apart three goats and a cow grazing nearby.

A short time later, Cripple Creek exploded in a riot as men smashed windows, broke into liquor warehouses, and drank more than they could hold. The Cripple Creek men were furious with Colorado Springs and their money, mine owners, the Republicans, and everyone else at the Springs. It turned into a good-sized disturbance.

The same men who blew up the Strong mine charged the Independence and forced twenty-one guards off the site and took control of the mine.

During this flurry of violence, John Calderwood, the union's organizer and stabilizer, had been out of the area speaking at union meetings around the state. When he came back, he talked "General" Johnson into leaving the district and jailed his top aide. Then he persuaded the men to settle down and asked the women to get their husbands home. Gradually the situation returned to a tense calm on Bull Mountain.

Sheriff Bowers decided he needed more men and hired another hundred gunmen from Denver and a hundred from Leadville. Stratton's mine had been seized by the strikers, and he urged Bowers to hire a whole regiment to deputize.

Before he was done, Sheriff Bowers hired 1,200 men and swore them in as deputies to go against the 700 striking miners on Bull Hill. He took his army by train to the Hayden Divide on the Colorado Midland railroad which is eighteen miles north of Cripple Creek and set up his field headquarters.

The president of Colorado College in the Springs, William S. Slocum, was sent to Altman to try to mediate the problem. He got nowhere with the miners, but did arrange to trade some prisoners who had been captured in skirmishes.

Governor Waite had been watching the situation and decided it was time he took charge. He went to Altman and talked with the miners and received their authority to be their arbitrator. Then he went back to the Springs and brought Calderwood and many of the mine owners together in a room at Colorado College and began the negotiations.

The mine owners were so irritated with Calderwood that he retreated to the hallway and let the governor mediate. After hours of pleading and shouting and threatening, the governor at last pounded out a settlement: The mine owners would agree to an eight-hour work day for three dollars, but they maintained their right to prosecute strike leaders and other strikers involved in criminal acts.

In the meantime, Sheriff Bowers had lost control of his hired gang of 1,200 camped at Hayden Divide. The men wanted some action, not just to be sitting there. They disowned the sheriff and chose Winfield Boynton as their leader. He had no military training—had been a shoe store clerk and a hotel man—but thought of himself as a military genius.

Boynton stirred up the men and convinced them he could lead them in a frontal attack on Bull Mountain and run the riffraff off and down the other side.

That's when Sheriff Bowers asked the governor for more state militiamen. He had to protect the 1,200 from getting shot to pieces by the entrenched 700 on Bull Mountain.

On June 6, 1894, the state militia, again under command of Attorney General Tarsney, left Denver for Cripple Creek by railroad.

At Hayden Divide, Boynton heard about it and knew what was happening. He roused his men and marched them south toward Altman. They landed in Beaver Park and pitched their tents. Boynton's plan was to charge up Bull Hill, chase the defenders off, and open it to the mine owners before the militia arrived.

His scouts reported no sign of armed men around Bull Hill three miles to the south. Boynton grinned. The rabble had heard he was coming and abandoned their trenches and scattered.

He assembled his men for a quick march up the hill to secure it once and for all.

The men marched a mile south, then were surprised with a sudden volley of rifle fire. The men went to the ground and soon saw that every rock and bush and tree and hump of ground ahead protected a rifle-firing striker. Most of the strikers were good with their weapons, and Boynton gave the order to fall back at once.

There is no document recording the dead or wounded in the melee, but the range precluded any heavy casualties. The men returned to Beaver Park and rested.

Boynton figured the defenders were busy congratulating themselves so he tried a night attack as soon as it got dark.

Many of the deputies got lost, some marched the wrong direction, and some began shooting at other deputies without knowing it. Another miserable failure by the irregular deputies.

Boynton took them back to Beaver Park. They remained there during June 7 and were still in their camp when Attorney General Tarsney marched in with his Colorado State Militia.

This time Tarsney used good sense and moved his men into Grassy Gulch in a direct line and between the strikers on Bull Hill and the hired deputy sheriffs at Beaver Park.

Boynton felt frustrated and angry. He needed to make a move to hold his troops. He divided his men into three units and sent them working around the edges of Bull Mountain. The only one to move up the hill was the Stratton brigade that went within a mile of the mountaintop.

The strikers responded by moving units forward. The militia quickly marched between the opposing forces and prevented a slaughter. General Tarsney ordered Sheriff Bowers to get the deputies off the hill. He did.

When the militia marched up Bull Mountain, they were welcomed by the strikers and turned over their weapons to the militia. The strike was over.

An agreement was signed June 10, 1894, at Altman. The rest of the strikers turned in their weapons and Sheriff Bowers disbanded his army of "deputies." It was agreed that the militia would stay until the mines were back to normal operations. The nine-hour-a-day mine owners agreed to go back to eight hours and the Strike of Ninety-Four was over. John Calderwood and 300 of his miners would surrender to stand trial.

Later in a trial, Calderwood was acquitted and only 2 of the 300 served any time, those for blowing up the Strong mine.

Historians say that the 130-day strike cost a little over $3 million in lost production, lost wages, cost of supporting the militia and paying and feeding the hired gunmen, and repairs to damaged mines.

With the strike behind them, the men and women of the Cripple Creek Mining District settled down to digging out all the gold they could and producing thirty more millionaires.

THE ANACONDA MINE, like most of the others in the Cripple Creek District, was shut down at least part of the time by the big miner strike of 1894. It was estimated the strike cost the state, the county, and the miners and mine owners over $3 million. (Photo Courtesy Colorado Springs Pioneer Museum)

FIFTEEN MILITIAMEN, a part of those sent in by the state of Colorado to maintain order during the Cripple Creek strike of 1894. The county sheriff recruited 1,200 "deputies" to go against the 700 dug-in miners on Bull Mountain. Luckily the three forces never fired more than a few shots at anyone. (Photo Courtesy Colorado Springs Pioneer Museum)

CHAPTER 12

Stratton and His Millions

Winfield Scott Stratton watched his empire grow from his cabin above Wilson Creek and close to his Independence mine. During 1894 and 1895 he took more than a million dollars a year from the mine, and he had no stockholders to pay. Some of the new mining millionaires in Cripple Creek rushed to Colorado Springs to buy fancy houses and try to move into high society, but not Stratton.

He worked a small crew and didn't push production. His Independence was much richer than the surrounding mines. His shafts were down only 250 feet by that time, and the workers were not even taking out all of the ore they could see.

Stratton evidently liked the security of it, knowing that there was plenty of gold there if he needed it.

Stratton refused to take on airs. He was still a working man with a job to get done, and he went about his way methodically doing it and earning his millions.

He refused to be impressed with himself, his accomplishments, or his great wealth. He did not hire expensive and hard-driving mining engineers to work his Independence. He relied on longtime friends who had "come up with him" in the Cripple Creek Bonanza.

Bob Schwartz, a former cobbler, was his general manager. Fred Trautman and Charlie Steel ran the Independence for him. Both were old friends.

For a while Stratton was a regular patron at some of the best parlour houses in Cripple Creek. Then the girls suggested for a man of his standing they should do something special. After that the girls visited Stratton in his cabin on a regular basis. He continued his usual hard drinking and gambling, often involving other nearby mine owners and friends Jimmie Burns and Jimmie Doyle and John Harnan of the Portland, J.R. McKinnie, and big Sam Strong.

Stratton was still the same man he had been when he first came to Cripple Creek. He was set in his ways, thin, tired, moody, often argumentative, and so pale he looked ill.

Work was his medicine.

The years 1893 to 1895 were good for Stratton. These were the times when he came the closest ever to being happy and fulfilled. He was rich, he could buy anything he wanted, he could travel, woo beautiful women, live in Paris or London. He did none of these.

He still preferred his solitary life in his Wilson Creek cabin some described as more of a shack. He took great joy in helping out the "tenderfeet" Irishmen to get the Portland on its feet and producing. The Portland wasn't nearly as rich as the Independence, but the Irish had a way of making it pay almost as much. They hired a large crew and bought the latest equipment to move more ore out of the ground and into the mills and smelters.

Stratton gave $20,000 to Colorado College in the Springs. He remembered his studies for a short time at the Colorado School of Mines at Golden and wrote them a draft for $25,000. He gave the Salvation Army $85,000 for some now unknown project, and showered Father Volpe with money to build his St. Peter's Church.

He did not short the Protestants either, with large amounts of cash going to the Presbyterian and Baptist churches. The Methodist tabernacle in Denver also received a more than generous donation.

When Stratton learned that many local citizens had lost money when they invested in the Washington claim under the early promotion of W.J. Wilcox, Stratton made it right. He repaid each person who had bought the now worthless Washington stock.

Stratton had no problem giving money away. It was because he didn't value it that much. He used it when it suited him to do good works and help folks. He stayed in his cabin on Wilson Creek until late 1895. The millionaires around him had left the hill long before, moving to the Springs and putting up or buying fancy mansions.

Many in the socially conscious Colorado Springs waited for Stratton to follow the other millionaires. They dreamed about the magnificent mansion that he would build with ballrooms and dozens of rooms, bedrooms and play rooms, and a tennis court and probably a stable for his fine Arabian horses.

They were all wrong. Late in 1895 Stratton did move to the Springs, but he didn't build a mansion. He didn't even buy one. J.R. McKinnie had a big house on North Weber Street. Sam Altman took over the large place previously owned by Count Pourtales. Even Jimmie Burns had his mansion on North Tejon Street.

Chapter 12

The whole town buzzed wondering where the biggest Cripple Creek gold rush millionaire of them all would light. He surprised them all and bought a plain frame house near downtown that he had built himself years before for Dr. Beverly Tucker. Stratton paid no attention whatsoever to the society ladies of the upper crust. He did however take an interest in politics since it was a presidential year.

It was the classical struggle of William Jennings Bryan against William McKinley. The Republicans scrambled to court Stratton and hoped that he would present them with a small token of his support, say $100,000. An emissary from Senator Ed Wolcott had a talk with Stratton and suggested that the party would be pleased to have his support. Stratton was noncommittal, but the messenger figured the contribution would be coming for sure.

Stratton had supported silver in the last election and lost. Now everyone figured with all of his gold wealth, he would come out for the gold standard, the Republicans, and William McKinley.

Again they were wrong. Shortly Stratton announced that he was supporting Bryan and that he had put up $100,000 in a deposit in the First National Bank of Colorado Springs as a bet on Bryan. He challenged anyone to cover his bet that Bryan would win. All they had to do was put up three-to-one odds and deposit $300,000 in the bank covering his bet.

The news of his bet made headlines in the capitols of Europe and all over the United States. Some thought it a strange bet. If Bryan won and re-established the silver standard at sixteen to one, it would mean Stratton's gold production would be worth exactly half of what he was then receiving.

Stratton made a statement available to the newspapers in which he said:

I do not make the offer because of any information that I have on the election, but I have a feeling that Bryan is going to win. I am deeply interested in seeing Bryan elected. I realize that the maintenance of the gold standard would perhaps be best for me individually, but I believe that free silver is the best thing for the working masses of this country. It is because I have a great respect for the intelligence and patriotism of the working people and I believe that they will see their duty at the polls that I am willing to make such an offer.

There should have been many takers. Bryan was considered a long shot at winning. Several people investigated the bet and the amount needed to cover it, but in the end, no one came forward with the $300,000. It would have been a good bet for the Republican National Party. When McKinley won and the bet was not challenged, Stratton got his deposit back.

Stratton had few close friends in the Springs. He seemed to prefer it that way. The old drinking buddies were busy being rich or off on junkets or buying sprees.

The one man Stratton enjoyed being with was the Springs lawyer who had saved the Portland mine for the Jimmies and Stratton back in 1893, Verner Reed. Stratton enjoyed talking and bantering with the man and admired his brilliance in business and the sometimes wild personality the man had developed.

The two often talked for hours in Stratton's office on Pike's Peak Avenue. They spoke of the Independence mine and about the adventures Reed had experienced in New Mexico with the Indians.

Chapter 12

Soon Reed traveled to Europe and to support himself there opened an office in London to sell Cripple Creek mining stocks. At the time, the Transvaal gold mines in South Africa were the big draw. Reed sold some local stocks and some mines to English groups. In his work, he met John Hays Hammond, the American mining genius. He had been kicked out of South Africa where he worked for Cecil Rhodes in the Rand. Later he joined a London firm called the Venture Corporation that invested in mines.

Reed cultivated Hammond, socialized with him, and soon learned that Hammond was worried that there was a real threat to the English control of the gold mines in South Africa. Hammond wanted to find a spectacular gold mine for which he could sell stock to English investors—if and when the bottom fell out in South Africa.

Reed knew the Independence better than anyone alive except Stratton. He sensed the chance of a big sale and began dropping bits of information and stories about the Independence bonanza so Hammond could hear them. Slowly Reed whetted Hammond's appetite until he was chafing at his mooring lines about the fabulous wealth and potential of the Independence.

With the bait cleverly placed, Reed went back to Cripple Creek and talked to Stratton. Reed told Stratton that he had the greatest chance for him to sell the Independence mine that had ever been heard of. The two men talked about it in the Pike's Peak office in the Springs.

Stratton asked his friend why he would want to sell the Independence.

Reed's response was because he could get Stratton more for the mine than any gold mine on earth had ever been sold for.

Stratton must have had a hard time believing a statement like that. As he pondered it, Reed took a fifty-dollar bill from his wallet and put it on Stratton's desk. He suggested a small wager. Reed would bet Stratton the fifty dollars that he would agree to sell the Independence within twenty-four hours.

Stratton knew a sure bet when he saw it. He laid his own fifty-dollar bill beside the other one.

Reed told Stratton that he'd been talking to John Hays Hammond, the American mining engineer who turned the Transvaal upside down. He'd been booted out of South Africa and was looking for a new bonanza. He was with a group in London called the Venture Corporation.

Stratton said he'd never heard of them. Hammond, of course, he knew about.

Reed said the Venture Corporation was interested in the Independence. If Hammond told them to buy, they would buy it. Then Reed dropped his bombshell. He told Stratton that he could sell the Independence for $10 million.

Ten million! It was enough money to take anyone by surprise. Stratton knew this wily salesman. If Reed said he could get ten million, it would be that much money in the bank.

To appreciate how much money that was in 1898, remember that the average wage for a miner was three dollars a day. Today the average working man earns about $100 a day or thirty-three times as much. With that basis, the ten million would have an equivalent today of about $330 million! It was an astounding amount of money, and it completely overwhelmed Stratton, who still thought of himself as a journeyman carpenter who knew how to build a cabinet or a house and could get the job done on time and within his budget.

The offer was one that not even Stratton could refuse. When Reed left Stratton's office later that same day, he had a written option to sell the Independence and the two fifty-dollar bills involved in the bet in his wallet.

Reed went back to London and put the deal in front of Hammond and the Venture Corporation. His price for the Independence to them was $11 million which included his commission of $1 million. Hammond was slightly interested but cool, saying the price was outrageous.

News from the Transvaal was bad, and Reed began to press the engineer, detailing the value of the mine. In the fall of 1898, Hammond asked if Reed could furnish him with an engineer's report on the Independence.

Reed hired T.A. Rickard, a mining engineer well-known to Hammond and one he trusted. Rickard's report was glowing. He said the mine was a true bonanza. His report showed that there was gold left to be mined in stopes and tunnels just waiting to be loaded up and taken to the smelter. He estimated the gold in sight was worth more than $7 million. The mine had been worked down only 700 feet, and some estimates were that gold bearing veins could be found in the Cripple Creek cauldron down to 3,000 feet. His final figures were the clincher.

Ore valued at $3,837,360 had been processed from the mine up to that point. That ore had resulted in a profit of $2,402,164 which was a profit of over 63 percent. Few mines anywhere in the world could meet that kind of a profit picture.

Hammond worried and wondered over the report of a bonanza of untold wealth in Cripple Creek. He stewed about it during the winter, and when Reed came to call in March of 1899 he was ready to bargain.

Stratton had continued as usual with no leak of the pending offer of the sale escaping. He went about his normal business and let it seem that he had no thought of selling the Independence.

Hammond tried to bargain with Reed, even threatening to buy other mines, but Reed knew of their value. He wore down the engineer, and at last Hammond recommended to the Venture Corporation that they buy the Independence for $11 million. Reed had closed the sale deal of the century and made himself a well-deserved $1 million.

It turned out to be a good investment. Before the Independence ran dry, the operators took out slightly more than $28 million in gold, far outstripping the $11 million price. One projection was wrong. The Independence didn't go down to 3,000 feet. It ran out of gold at 1,420 feet.

When news of the sale hit the U.S., no one in Cripple Creek or in the Springs believed it.

Stratton went to London in the spring of 1899 and signed over the Independence to the Venture Corporation. He was not in the best of health and took his doctor, David Rice, along with him. Stratton had long suffered diabetes and liver trouble from his bouts with strong drink.

He had medical treatments in Vienna. He brought over a friend, Bob Schwartz, to translate the German for him. Later they visited Switzerland to see Bob's sister. Stratton bought her a house and gave her $20,000. He spent time in Paris and didn't enjoy it much. By August of 1899 he was ready to come home.

His health was no better than when he left. Now he had spells of depression and despair. He saw greed and big money break up the partnership of the two Jimmies who had found the Portland mine. At times he felt great wealth was more a curse than a blessing.

The depression led to more drinking which hurt his health even more.

In the late days of the century, Stratton concentrated on giving away his money. For Christmas of 1899 he gave each of his key employees at his mines a present of $50,000.

Seven other employees were gifted with new homes. One day he saw Bob Womack walking slowly past his office looking beaten and in pain. Stratton gave him $5,000.

He had erected a five-story building for the Colorado Mining Exchange and gave it to them free of charge.

In a sudden splurge, he bought $2 million worth of real estate in Denver including a huge mortgage on the famous Brown Palace Hotel.

In quick order he spent almost $5 million after his return from Europe. All of this money had come out of his accounts and income from other sources. He hadn't spent a dime of the ten million from his sale of the Independence.

Forever the prospector, Stratton yearned for a project that he could really get involved with. He remembered the theory that the gold veins in Cripple Creek had been birthed a mile down in the center of the cauldron. He examined a study of the angles of the veins and decided that the theory was right.

A mile down under Cripple Creek, the gold veins had been created from a fantastically rich, huge lake of gold. It would be a hundred, maybe five hundred times as rich as the Independence.

Stratton picked the spot to begin digging, a claim called the Plymouth Rock near the top of Ironclad Hill. He already had some claims in the area. Now he bought more. Soon he was spending $10,000 a day buying up worthless claims.

In a few weeks he owned more than a hundred claims in the area and about six hundred acres of real estate. Before he was done at Ironclad Hill, he had spent $8 million on the project that never produced a dollar's worth of gold.

The infusion of Stratton gold into the Cripple Creek economy was a boom to the whole area. Stratton didn't mind spending the money. It was done in Cripple Creek, the town that had been good to him, and for a few months it gave him pleasure.

The depression came over him again, the black moods that left him wondering what good he had done by being rich. What was the use of anything? He wondered if the Cripple Creek Bonanza had actually done anyone any good. He scowled and stared out his office window and knew that almost none of those thirty Cripple Creek millionaires were happy.

In 1897 Stratton had watched with some pleasure as the Woods brothers, Frank and Harry, were doing well. Their Gold Coin mine had produced rich ore and they had formed the town of Victor. He couldn't think of anybody in the district who was more honest than the Woods brothers. They helped out their miners who fell on hard times or got into trouble. They paid the top wages in the district and even built an amusement park for the town.

During 1898 Stratton saw the Woods brothers' fortunes expand as they created a transport tunnel to haul out their ore from the Gold Coin, then built a half-million-dollar chlorination plant at Arequa Gulch and a half-million-dollar hydroelectric power system to run their tram cars in the Gold Coin.

Stratton saw the men change from benevolent to grasping and greedy, as they tried to gobble up the whole camp. He knew they were overextending themselves and their house would come down.

In 1900 the profits from the Gold Coin began to decline and fire destroyed most of the Victor downtown area. The fortunes of the Wood brothers were in a serious downturn.

By 1902 Stratton spent most of his time in his Weber Street house at the Springs. He was confined to his bed and a chair. He read a lot and relied on his constant companion, the quart of whiskey that he drank each day. He was not an old man. Come July of 1902 he would be fifty-four years old. He looked and felt as if he was a hollow shell just waiting to die.

He knew two trades, prospecting and carpentry. He had been successful at both. He had behaved well, treated all men with fairness and charity. He had been poor and he had been rich. He had been a celebrity to some degree and a lowly for-hire carpenter.

But he admitted to himself that he had never truly been a happy man. Why?

Three years before he had written a will that was kept a secret. He knew the will would make the townspeople gasp in surprise. It was one, though, that helped sustain him the last three years of his life.

He sat in his house and grew weaker and more frail by the day. His liver was almost ruined, but it gave him no pain. He went into a coma on September 13, 1902. Bob Schwartz, his bootmaker and German translator, came and sat with him in the Weber Street house. For a brief moment that evening, Stratton came out of the coma and talked with Bob. He lapsed back into the coma and died on September 14, 1902.

He was eulogized in newspapers throughout the world as the greatest of the millionaires ever to have gold fever. Two days after his death, he lay in the Mining Exchange and over 9,000 people came to pay their last respects. The next day he was buried in the Springs' Evergreen cemetery facing Pike's Peak and on a wooded knoll. Later many more of Cripple Creek's millionaires found final peace on that knoll.

A week after Stratton's death, the will was read. He left a total of a half million dollars to various nephews and nieces and to the son he had by an early and unhappy marriage.

There was $6 million left in his estate, and he ordered that it be used to set up and maintain a home for poor children and old people. It was to be called the Myron Stratton Home, named after his father.

The home was built to Stratton's specifications. The children were given every advantage that rich children enjoyed. The elderly lived in individual cottages, and the place had no resemblance to an institution. It had handsome buildings, lawns, a swimming pool, tennis courts, and pleasant avenues bordered with cottages.

It opened in 1914 on land near Cheyenne Mountain and housed 100 children and 100 elderly residents. The first few years its budget was $200,000 a year.

Some say that Cripple Creek's greatest days ended when Winfield Scott Stratton died in 1902. It was the peak year of gold production, with $19 million taken from the ground in the Cripple Creek Mining District. Some of the parlour houses were closing. Some of the stores and hotels were in decline.

Now Stratton had died, the man who had dumped $8 million into the economy of Cripple Creek on a worthless venture. He had been trying to give back to his small town part of his wealth.

In his Springs boarding house, Bob Womack heard about the passing and must have nodded. "Poor Old Man Stratton, all that money to worry about. I don't envy him one bit."

CHAPTER 13

Rails to Cripple Creek

So many of the good developments in Cripple Creek owed their start to Winfield Scott Stratton. Early on Stratton realized that to be most productive, Cripple Creek needed rail transportation. Wagons worked to get the ore eighteen miles to the rail siding at Florissant, but a rail line looping around the gold fields with a siding at every mine would be so much better.

He knew Harry Collbran, the general manager of the Colorado Midland Railroad which ran from the Springs to Florissant and points beyond. Every chance he had, Stratton pointed out to Collbran what a moneymaker a branch line from Midland's siding at Hayden Divide to the gold mines at the Cripple Creek District would be.

After a few months of Stratton pestering him in early 1893, Collbran talked to his corporate owners, the giant Santa Fe Railroad. The big line looked at the proposal and decided they didn't want to make the investment to push the eighteen-mile spur across the mountains and down into Cripple Creek.

By that time, Stratton had Collbran so fired up about the project that he decided to go ahead and do the branch line on his own. Harlan P. Lillibridge was a Springs millionaire with not much to do, and Collbran talked to him about the project and soon received $100,000 to push the railroad into Cripple Creek.

W. K. Gillett, the passenger auditor of the Santa Fe line, liked the idea, even if his bosses didn't, and told Collbran he thought it was a workable plan. If it came about, then Santa Fe would pick up a lot of business both from freight and passengers.

Collbran started his railroad construction. He had the knowhow and hired engineers who knew what they were doing, and by September of 1893 they had nine miles of narrow gauge track laid down from Hayden Divide south toward Cripple Creek. The problem was Collbran had underestimated and had run out of money.

He also knew that he had competition.

Earlier there had been the start of a railroad aimed at Cripple Creek from the south. Dave Moffit began it in Florence and worked north up a steep ravine called Eight Mile Canyon to Phantom Canyon. He would build from there into Victor and on to Cripple Creek. It would be a run of forty miles on a narrow gauge track.

The line was tough to build, went over steep winding grades, and made a climb from 5,187 feet up to just over 10,000 feet.

One delay came after another. It was a hard road to build and would prove to be an even harder one to maintain with washouts and rockslides on the rugged route.

Collbran realized that the Moffit road would have an advantage over his. The Florence & Cripple Creek railroad was narrow gauge, and it would connect at Florence with the Denver and Rio Grande, which was also a narrow gauge. No freight reloading would be required, and cars could switch directly to the northbound tracks at Florence.

Collbran's narrow gauge, on the other hand, would connect with the standard gauge Colorado Midland at Hayden Divide, and ore would have to be unloaded from the narrow gauge cars and put on the wider tracked cars. Passengers also would have to change trains to board the cars for the run on into the Springs.

Collbran went back to his "angel" and asked for another $100,000 to finish his railroad. Lillibridge listened to his plea and turned him down. To him it may have looked like this new line was too little and too late.

Collbran didn't bother going back to the Santa Fe officials, knowing they wouldn't help. He and Gillett decided to go into partnership and switch the nine miles of track to standard gauge and push it on into Cripple Creek. They would find their financing somehow.

If it happened today, both men would be thrown in jail for fraud, conspiracy, and grand theft. In 1893 and 1894 the economy was slow; many of the workers on the Colorado Midland had little to do. Because of their executive status, Collbran and Gillett used idle Colorado Midland company men to work on building their private railroad, the Midland Terminal.

The Colorado Midland had 350 miles of track. Collbran went on a trip and found large quantities of unused materials he deemed to be "defective." This included sizable amounts of ties, lumber for trestles, tanks, switches, spikes, rails, and even tools. The "defective" material was loaded on cars for "disposal" and promptly shipped to Hayden Divide and used on the Midland Terminal project.

This couldn't happen for long without the top officials in the Santa Fe and Colorado Midland finding out about it. They didn't complain because they knew if the project was a success, then both their lines would get a great deal of increased business and at a nominal cost. They were paying the men anyway, and the materials would not be missed.

It took the Midland Terminal railroad workers until January 1, 1894 to revamp the first six miles of the old road into a standard gauge line. They had come to what they called the Midland Station.

Now they had their line open for six miles. Freight shipments bound for Cripple Creek now could go by way of Midland Station and be closer to Cripple Creek than if they offloaded at Florissant. Stagecoaches and wagons met the trains at Midland and rushed the people and freight to Cripple Creek.

The Colorado Midland line loaned a dozen trains to the fledging line and they began making the twelve runs a day to Midland Station.

Now came the hard part, the uphill grades that would take them up to the 10,000-foot level and down into Cripple Creek. Their engineers projected that this part, another twelve miles, would cost at least $70,000 a mile to build.

Cash money was the problem now. They couldn't borrow materials to make this part. They needed workers and earth moving equipment and time to build the grades up the mountains.

All the while, Dave Moffat's Florence & Cripple Creek line kept pushing up the steep grades toward the mining district. Collbran watched the progress with one eye and worried about his own project with the other.

Gillett came to the rescue. Large shipments were now coming to Cripple Creek to the Midland Station. Gillett made it a policy to collect the entire shipping charge when the goods hit Midland Station. Usually about 95 percent of the freight charges were due to other railroads all over the country.

The same way, when freight was shipped out of Midland Station or passengers took trips from there, the road collected the entire charges for the trip or for the freight. Again, most of this money was due and payable to the other participating rail lines.

Gillett used all of the proceeds from both these operations to foot the construction of the last part of the Midland Terminal railroad. Accounts between railroads were usually supposed to be paid within ninety days. Records show that Gillett didn't pay many of the accounts with the other railroads for as long as five years.

Through the spring of 1894 the two roads kept at their construction.

The Midland Terminal had an easier route to cover, going from an altitude of 9,183 feet at Divide to a height of 9,500 feet at Cripple Creek. The downgrades from Divide resulted in a rise in the roadbed of just over 2,000 feet.

The Florence and Cripple Creek line had a much tougher road to build with a rise of just over 5,000 feet during the forty miles of track laying.

Soon, Collbran realized that the Florence line would get into Cripple Creek before his own tracks. He gritted his teeth and went back to working harder.

It was a big celebration when, on July 1 or July 2 depending on your source, the Florence & Cripple Creek railway steamed into Cripple Creek.

A huge crowd met the hissing and puffing steam engine. The great day had arrived. Now Cripple Creek was tied into the outside world by a pair of steel rails. Now there would be no end of modern improvements. The narrow gauge line immediately made hauling deals with the mines in Poverty Gulch and Gold Hill.

The road became known as the "Gold Belt Line" and soon put on passenger trains that ran from Cripple Creek to Florence three times a day. In Florence the road connected with the Denver and Rio Grande, which was also a narrow gauge. This meant that no gold ore or other freight or passengers would have to switch trains to continue.

Quickly the Florence & Cripple Creek put on Pullman service that ran between Cripple Creek and Denver. True, the passengers did have to go south forty miles to Florence and then back northeast over fifty-three more miles to get to Colorado Springs, a total of ninety-three miles.

The new route on the Midland Terminal would be only fifty-five miles. But the Midland Terminal line was not yet built into Cripple Creek.

The Florence & Cripple Creek took advantage of its monopoly as long as it could. The line had as many as fifty-eight passenger trains running between Cripple Creek and Victor every day.

The overnight to Denver left Cripple Creek each night at nine o'clock. At one-thirty A.M. a Pullman-equipped train left Colorado Springs heading for Cripple Creek. Now the swells who could afford it could travel in comfort and luxury to Colorado Springs or all the way to Denver.

The narrow gauge line set up a new wholly owned company that extended from Victor into the rich mining fields nearby to pick up more ore shipments. The cars had only to be switched on board the Florence tracks and they were off to the smelter and mills.

At the height of its labors, the Florence & Cripple Creek had almost 300 freight cars and 16 passenger coaches.

The line has been called one of the most successful railroads in the nation's history. It paid its construction costs of

$800,000 during the first year of operation. It had six months more to pile up profits before the Midland Terminal line reached Cripple Creek.

When it came in, Collbran and Gillett saw that there were a lot of rich mines on the east slopes of Bull Hill. They ran their line that way and tied up the rest of the Cripple Creek ore business.

The route of the Midland Terminal went west up Ute Pass over the Colorado Midland line as far as Divide. There it turned south for Gillett through the range of mountains. Next it went on to Cameron over Victor Pass and then into Victor. From there the tracks snaked into Elkton and Anaconda. At last it came to the three-story brick depot at the foot of Bennett Avenue in Cripple Creek.

The long loop around Cripple Creek by the Midland Terminal line was finished in December of 1895. It was a serious blow to the fortunes of the Florence & Cripple Creek. Now the Midland Terminal had the best ore deposits. Add to that the fact that due to washouts and steep grades, the Florence & Cripple Creek line was much more expensive to operate than its rival.

With gold ore processing mills opening in Colorado Springs, the haul route to the Springs via the Midland Terminal was almost half as long.

Four years later, Moffat gave up on his sinking ship and sold the stock of the Florence & Cripple Creek RR to the Midland Terminal.

The line itself continued to operate on a reduced basis until 1912 when a cloudburst hit Phantom Canyon and washed away nine miles of the right-of-way and smashed eighteen bridges into rubble.

As soon as the Midland Terminal line arrived in 1895, it set up passenger service as well as ore hauling. The M-T ran four passenger trains every day between Cripple Creek and

Colorado Springs. The run one way took two hours and cost
$2.50 for a round trip ticket. Remember, $2.50 was almost
a full day's wages for a working miner back then. The "Cripple Creek Flyer" was the name of the train that offered daily
Pullman service from Cripple Creek all the way to Denver.
It was quicker, easier, and less expensive than the same destination on the Florence & Cripple Creek line and further
depleted the other rail line's ability to compete.

The Midland Terminal railroad was a money maker. It
had position, the best route, and a virtual monopoly on the
gold ore hauling job out of Cripple Creek. The ore was transported down the hill to Colorado Springs where mills had
been built to process it.

When the Carlton mill was built in the district in 1949,
the need for the long haul ended, and the ore was processed
locally. That was the death knell for the Midland Terminal
line. Late in 1949 the railroad closed down and passed into
history.

The third rail line into Cripple Creek didn't arrive until
1901 when the Colorado Springs & Cripple Creek District
railroad steamed its way into Cripple Creek.

The line was built by mine owners looking for their own
route to send ore to the mills in Colorado Springs and cut
out the profit of the middle man railroad.

The line, forty-six miles long, nine miles shorter than
the Midland Terminal, charged up out of Colorado Springs
directly into the mountains heading for the gold fields. The
standard gauge road cost $4.6 million to build and was considered an extraordinary accomplishment of railroad engineering.

The line quickly became a tourist attraction because of
the spectacular scenery and the rugged ride up through the
mountains.

It served the mine owners of the day who had over 60 ore cars, 18 passenger cars, and 4 observation cars. They boasted of 8 eighty-five-ton locomotives and 4 switch engines as well as 225 boxcars. Records show that in 1902 more than 50,000 tourists took the trip up the mountain on the Colorado Springs & Cripple Creek District Railway.

The new route to the Springs brought competition for the passenger dollar. The Midland Terminal dropped its fare to $2 a round trip, then down to $1.50 and soon to $1. The low ball bidding continued until the lines had lowered their round trip fare from the Springs to Cripple Creek to a quarter. A truce ended the price war and the ticket costs moved back to more reasonable levels.

The "short line" was like a beautiful flower. It bloomed gloriously for four years, then money problems came up and the mine owners didn't want to spend any more cash on the line. It was sold just before it went into receivership. The Colorado & Southern railroad bought it and at once leased it to the Midland Terminal. The short line to Cripple Creek went out of business in 1920.

The addition of the first two railroads to Cripple Creek assured the mine owners of economical transportation for their ore, and that paved the way for the continued success of the Cripple Creek Bonanza. The railroads were the heart of the gold mining district.

When the Carlton mill was built in Cripple Creek and there was no more need for the railroads to haul ore, most of the tracks were torn up. Later the grades were used for roads and highways. Today, driving to Cripple Creek from the Springs, you can follow either of the former railroad line grades on paved highways.

ORE CAR RAILS like these were in every tunnel in the district. The ore cars on them hauled out worthless rock as well as gold ore. The split in the tunnel here is unusual. The tunnels followed the course of the gold veins. (Photo Courtesy Pikes Peak Library District)

THE FIRST FLORENCE & CRIPPLE CREEK train pulls into Victor on July 2, 1894. This Engine 92, a baggage car, and the two coaches were all leased from the Denver and Rio Grande. The trains brought new services and new means of transporting ore and boosted the mining in the Cripple Creek District. (Photo Courtesy Cripple Creek District Museum)

MIDLAND TERMINAL RAILROAD CAME into Cripple Creek in December of 1895 to this brick depot at the foot of Bennett Avenue. Pictured are the conductor, the engineer, fireman, the brakeman, and depot manager. (Photo Courtesy Cripple Creek District Museum)

DEVIL'S SLIDE C.S. & C.C. SHORT LINE.

THE SHORT LINE became an instant tourist attraction for its spectacular scenery. It arrived in Cripple Creek in 1901. Here a three-car train passes the Devil's slide. On the roadway below can be seen a two-horse rig going uphill the hard way. (Photo Courtesy Pikes Peak Library District)

CHAPTER 14

The Law and Disorder

The first few years of the Cripple Creek Bonanza there was little crime in the district. This was not a wild and wide-open placer mining area where a thousand dollars in gold dust might be in a miner's tent, or a stretch of rich placer claim might be contested by two miners with knives, guns, and shovel handles. Gold here was deep in the earth and it took patience, luck, and a lot of development money to make any strike pay out that first ounce of pure gold.

Most of the early miners at Cripple Creek were not traditional prospectors, but carpenters, plumbers, laborers, and even dentists from Colorado Springs. These men had a history of being steady, law-abiding citizens.

During 1893, when the big money came to Cripple Creek and the wealth of the mines spread, the influx of the mining camp fast buck guys, the prostitutes, the con-men and the shady characters, as well as a hardened criminal element all began looking for a cut of the golden pie. The bad apple migration to Cripple Creek grew with each year.

The first recorded murder in Cripple Creek happened in 1892 when a Negro ex-convict tried to vent his anger against a bartender in the Ironclad Dance Hall. His revolver shot missed his target and killed Reuben Miller, who worked there as the piano player.

In 1891 and 1892 law enforcement in Cripple Creek was in the hands of the El Paso County deputy sheriff, Peter Eales. His main concern was Colorado Springs, but Cripple Creek was part of El Paso County at that point and within his jurisdiction.

Cripple Creek was a train ride and then an eighteen-mile stagecoach ride from the Springs, so law enforcement was often on an "as needed" basis. In fact there was little lawman work to do in the district since the criminal elements had not charged into the district yet. Many times the law work involved only the settling of disputes in saloons and chastising the soiled doves when they tried to entice customers in public places.

The repeal of the Sherman Act in late 1893 caused Cripple Creek a lot of trouble and also did it a lot of good. When the act first was passed, it put the country on the silver standard and authorized the government to buy 4.5 million ounces of silver each month. The repeal stopped that purchase. Colorado had dozens of silver mines that had contributed greatly to the state's prosperity. Now the price of silver slumped, and without the government buy, the silver price crashed. The price dropped by half and most of the silver mines shut down.

This threw out of work thousands of hard rock miners. With the digs in Cripple Creek booming, thousands of the out-of-work miners flocked into Cripple Creek looking for work.

Few of the miners found work, but a lot stayed, and these idle men meant more problems for law enforcement.

The worst violence in the small town's history came in 1894 when the miners struck the mine owners for three dollars a day wages for eight hours of work. This resulted in beatings, fires, explosions, and confrontations of hundreds of armed forces and the deployment of a thousand men from the Colorado militia on orders from the governor.

After the 130-day strike was over, things settled down a little, but a lot of the strike breakers and gunmen, brought in to fight the battle, stayed in Cripple Creek, and these men made a big difference in the crime element in the district.

Cripple Creek tried to meet force with force by electing to office some hard cases who they hoped could deal with the riffraff left over from the union fight.

Bob Mullen, one of the men who had been a leader of the army of "deputies" sworn in by the El Paso County sheriff, was elected to the office of Cripple Creek police magistrate.

A man with a criminal past, Jim Marshall, became the Cripple Creek town marshal. For two years this pair ran roughshod over the rights of many citizens of Cripple Creek with the sanction of the city council, which evidently decided that you couldn't make a good omelet without breaking some eggs.

Then in July of 1896 the pair stepped over the line a little too far when the police arrested a preacher and his wife. Little publicity was given the arrest, but many people came to the trial. Not even the charges are known now. Rex Mollette, an attorney in town who had been busy denouncing corruption in the city administration, heard of the arrest and went to the trial.

He was met at the door by two deputies who told Mollette he couldn't come in. He said it was his right to enter, and the deputies beat him up and hauled him off to jail.

Police magistrate Mullen found Mollette guilty on a disorderly conduct charge and fined him a hundred dollars.

That was a month's wages for a working man. Mollette needed medical attention after the beating but was not allowed any and was denied bail and kept in jail until the magistrate decided to release him.

The incident provoked anger among the town's leading businessmen and property owners. They sent around a petition asking for an investigation of the town's officials. One of the petitioners, attorney George Bently, was quickly arrested for violating a bill-posting ordinance. The magistrate fined him and refused to let him out of jail on bail.

In 1896 the good people of Cripple Creek were fed up with their marshal and magistrate. The newly formed Municipal Reform League heard of the second arrest and began a wide investigation of the police department and other offices of the town's officials. The highly active Cripple Creek Bar Association gave its support to the investigation.

With this and pressure from other leading citizens, Mayor Steele held a meeting of the town's board of trustees. He was going to suggest that consideration be given to the suggestions by the civic organizations, but he couldn't. Only three of the six trustees attended, which meant there was no quorum so no business could be transacted. At least two of the trustees were known to be close friends of the Marshall and Mullen team and stayed away on purpose.

The Municipal League conducted an audit of the town's financial records.

A few days later, a story appeared in the Denver newspapers as a result of the probe. The paper stated that figures showed that Marshal Jim Marshall had stolen between $20,000 and $30,000 in city funds. The bank account showed a balance of only $17,000, which the paper said indicated strongly that much more money must have been stolen. The paper said they had complaints from gambling houses that had to pay a large amount of cash each month so they could operate twenty-four hours a day.

The paper stipulated that monthly licenses for gambling devices and prostitutes should have netted the city over $30,000 a year in revenue. Marshal Marshall, responsible for collecting such monies, had turned over only $5,081 in 1895. This left over $25,000 that was unaccounted for. Other city officials were also thought to be embezzling money. Sixty-five saloons in town that year paid $600 each in license fees. That was $39,000 that should be on the books. An audit showed only $29,000 had been recorded as credited to saloon revenues. The committee decided that there had been a total of more than $40,000 stolen by town officials during that year.

Judge Mullen was charged by the committee of making no attempt to be just or fair in court cases. Almost all defendants were not allowed to have a lawyer with them. Usually their testimony was ridiculed and ignored.

One such case involved a washwoman who did laundry for the city clerk. She complained that the clerk had not paid her for her work. The clerk charged the woman with keeping a "dirty" house, and the judge refused to listen to her defense or the charges against the clerk. She was fined fifty dollars and put in jail.

The committee charged the marshal with running a lice-infested jail with no sanitary facilities. The committee said that Marshall had a torture chamber in his jail. He put an iron box in the building next to the heating stove. Then he built a fire in the stove and locked a victim in the iron box. The hotter the iron box became the more readily the person inside charged with a crime would confess, whether he was guilty or not.

One time a German immigrant was arrested for carrying a concealed weapon. In reality it was an antique pistol wrapped in a handkerchief. Judge Mullen fined him fifty dollars plus another seven dollars in court costs—which was exactly the amount of cash the man had in his wallet.

Mullen moved into higher financial levels. Two saloon owners were accused of selling liquor without a license. The two men had a lease on property owned by friends of the judge who wanted the property back so they could put up a brick building.

The two men showed the judge a written receipt for their license payment. Judge Mullen ruled that the written receipt was not proof of payment and ordered the saloon men evicted from the leased building and put in jail.

While the saloon men tried to get out of jail, a group of Cripple Creek police ripped down the frame building and piled the resulting trash and wood in the middle of the street.

Pressure mounted from all sides, and on August 4, 1896 proceedings began against Police Magistrate Mullen before the city council. Rex Mollette told how he was assaulted and jailed and tried illegally. After a dozen witnesses testified against Mullen, the meeting recessed.

The trial of Mullen continued on August 7. Again testimony was given of the judge's bad conduct. This time the pressure put on the city council by the Municipal League paid off.

Judge Mullen was suspended by a unanimous vote, pending a complete investigation. Mullen was not present. It was the last time that Mullen gets any attention in the press of the day and we assume that he faded from the scene with his ill-gotten gains.

The marshal was a tougher case to handle. A special committee of the Municipal League worked to come to a final tally on the city's financial records. Many had been burned in the fire of 1894. The marshal said simply that his records had been stolen by person or persons unknown.

However, from the two years of records, they uncovered one after another case of fines paid and not reported, of names not on lists of those who were licensed, and other irregularities that spelled fraud for sure.

The information was taken to the grand jury in the Springs. The twelve men worked over the evidence for two weeks. The prosecuting attorney said that no honest man could fail to indict the marshal.

On September 23, 1896 the grand jury found for the defendant saying that there was insufficient evidence to indict him. The *Cripple Creek Times* reported that Marshall had been in the Springs during the whole two weeks of the deliberations and openly charged Marshall with bribery and intimidation of witnesses called by the grand jury. It also accused the grand jury of whitewashing the whole affair.

Marshall was back at his old stand again and efforts to oust him seemed to have failed.

Then on November 5 the city council held its regular meeting. That night the legal firm of Thompson, Perking and Thompson gave petitions to the city council demanding the suspension of Marshall and his chief deputy, Thomas Clark. The petitions stated that the two men had threatened to kill county sheriff's deputies L.S. Lambert and D.W. Clark if they continued certain of their duties of arresting suspected law breakers. In another statement, city police officer William Finch testified that he had been told not to interfere with or arrest a group of armed robbers because they were friends of the marshal.

The case was continued to the next week and then continued again and moved to a larger hall. On November 11 the meeting began in the Exchange Building, but because the structure was unheated the case had to be postponed again.

The last hearing on the case was held back in the city council chambers. It started in the morning and lasted all day and into the night. After a short time of deliberations, the councilmen voted four to two to suspend the two top lawmen permanently.

For the next few years the law and order procedures became more normal and served the people rather than the other way around in Cripple Creek.

However in early times and later years, strong sheriffs were often the rule of the day in Cripple Creek, as in many other Western towns.

One story is that the sheriff of Teller County (after it had been formed with Cripple Creek as county seat) had some friends who ran an illegal still back in the hills. One day the sheriff was riding near the place when he met a wounded man stumbling along the road. The man worked at the still and knew the sheriff, and he told him that some armed gang had come in and beat up the crew, shot some of them, and was stealing the still and the whiskey.

The sheriff thanked the man, then slipped around the hill to a spot where he had cover and used his rifle to pick off the robbers one at a time. When all of them were dead, he went down to the spot, loaded up the wagon with the seven dead men, and headed down the road toward Colorado Springs.

Every mile along the route he pitched off one of the bodies of the robbers until all seven had been discarded.

The report was that nobody ever bothered that still again.

Some sources say that this particular sheriff was a stay-at-home kind of a man. He had good reason. He never left Teller County because he knew there were arrest warrants for murder out on him in many of the surrounding counties. There's no record of what happened to this colorful Cripple Creek sheriff.

EARLY CRIPPLE CREEK showing telegraph poles on the left and the tinder-dry wooden buildings crowded along the street. This was taken prior to the fire of 1895 and shows the dirt street, the boardwalks in front of stores, but no depot at the end of the street. (Photo Courtesy Colorado Springs Pioneer Museum)

CHAPTER 15

Firestorm Disaster

Early Cripple Creek was a firetrap waiting to happen. The town was built of thin pine boards, sawed out one day and nailed up the next into houses, saloons, stores, and gambling halls. The green lumber dried out, cracked, seasoned, and warped, and over three or four years became tinder dry.

All that was needed was a spark or flame to set it off. That flame came on a quiet Saturday morning, April 25, 1896. The weather was warm for April, and the last of the snow that fell two weeks before had melted off roofs and out of ditches and side streets.

A spring wind blew in from Victor and helped dry out the ground, and the new life of spring was in the air.

A bartender went to see his lady friend, who had a rented room over the Central Dance Hall on the corner of Myers and Third Street. He climbed the steps and went into her room. She was getting ready for her work downstairs as a taxi dancer. No one knows exactly what it was all about, but soon an argument erupted between the two.

The argument turned into a shouting match and the bartender slapped the woman. She grabbed a Bowie knife and charged him. The man caught her arm to avoid the arc of the honed blade, and as he jolted backward, his foot kicked over the lighted kerosene heater that was chasing the last chill of the night from the room.

At once the flaming liquid spread across the floor. The two tried to put out the fire, but it ate hungrily at the dry wood, and after a minute or two they must have realized that the fire was out of control. They rushed down the steps and gave the alarm.

A few minutes later Fire Chief Allen called out the volunteer firemen with three shots from his revolver. The fire spread so quickly in the Central Dance Hall rooms that a few of the dance hall hostesses living on the third floor had to slide down ropes that firemen threw up to them. The whole building exploded into flames.

By this time in its development, Cripple Creek had a water system, and the firemen used hoses for a half hour to try to confine the blaze to the dance hall. After the half hour, they had drained down the reservoir and the pressure dropped, making the hoses useless.

Now the fire surged forward like a living thing, eating everything in its way.

The south wind whipped up harder, and embers from the Central Dance Hall carried across Myers Avenue. There the Topic Dance Hall caught fire. The two-story Topic gushed into flames and the firemen had no water to stop it.

Within minutes the Victor Fire Department volunteers arrived, but there was little they could do. The flames from the Topic jumped across the alley and ate into the back of the stores that fronted on Bennett Avenue.

One way to stop a fire is with a fire break to create an area where there is no fuel. Firemen began creating one in Cripple Creek. They dynamited the shacks on the east side of Third Street for 200 feet between Myers and Bennett avenues. This shut down the blaze from spreading west.

The flames surged north and east ravaging everything on Bennett Avenue between Third and Fourth. The mining exchange roared into flames, Johnnie Nolon's saloon burned, the First National Bank and then the post office all fell to the surging firestorm of flames.

Forty homes on Carr and Eaton avenues burned in the holocaust and then the flames turned east to Fifth Street and attacked the Midland Terminal depot. Myers Avenue cribs and shacks between Fifth and Third caught the brunt of the last surge of the fire before it died when the wind quieted. The flames stopped almost where they had started.

The Butte Opera House was gone, along with Marie Pappalan's Abbey Saloon and dozens of business places.

In a frantic three hours, the fire leveled thirty acres of buildings and houses and 1,500 people were without homes. The mayor, Hugh Steele, named a committee to get housing for those burned out.

Some of the Cripple Creekers began rebuilding before the ashes had cooled. George Jordan and Joe Finley, who had owned the My Fried Saloon on Myers Avenue, built a ten-by-twelve-foot shack on the edge of the street in front of their still smoking saloon. They began serving drinks on an oilcloth-covered plank bar by eight o'clock Saturday night.

The Cripple Creek *Times* came out with its usual Sunday edition after moving from its fire-ravaged quarters to new digs at a small printing shop on Golden Avenue.

Johnnie Nolon began getting lumber Saturday to rebuild his saloon.

Kittie Townley hired twenty men Sunday morning, and they began building one-girl cribs.

Life would go on in Cripple Creek.

Monday and Tuesday were clean-up time with more plans to rebuild. The fire chief estimated the dollar loss of the fire at $500,000 with no more than one fourth of that covered by fire insurance.

Wednesday dawned bright and clear again, and work continued on the rebuilding process. The couple who started the fire was questioned and not charged, since the fire began accidentally.

Wednesday afternoon, April 29, 1896, another fire began in the Portland Hotel at the corner of Myers and Second Street. The building had gone up in 1891 as the Window Hotel but had fallen into disrepair. A fire started in the hotel's kitchen when a pan of grease spilled on a hot kitchen range.

This spring day the southerly wind came at Cripple Creek with much stiffer force than it had during the last fire and the evidence of it was soon at hand.

The fire in the Portland Hotel exploded out of control, and the old hotel burned with a fury that sent a roaring sound over all of Cripple Creek. The roof of the hotel fell in just before three in the afternoon, and that caused burning embers to shower northward halfway up Mount Pisgah. The burning brands and coals fell on house roofs and stores and businesses and started dozens of new blazes. The Palace Hotel at Bennett Avenue and Second Street caught fire and sent flames a hundred feet into the air. Soon the boilers in the hotel exploded and injured six firefighters who were trying to control the blaze.

A few minutes later another explosion rocked the town as 700 pounds of dynamite detonated in the Harder Grocery on Myers Avenue.

The wind whipped the fire as one block after another fell to the flames. Firefighters tried to dynamite fire breaks, but it did no good as the flames jumped even one hundred feet of leveled houses or buildings and raced onward.

Men, women, and children rushed from the streets to some spot of safety. The closest one was up the hill and around the reservoir at the end of town. Women and children clustered there waiting for word about their homes and their husbands who were below trying to fight the fire.

The hard-blowing wind whipped the flames, sending fire brands hundreds of feet ahead to start new fires. At last there was nothing the firefighters could do except get out of the way of the marching walls of flames.

Stores and businesses and banks and churches and homes all fell in the wake of the surging massive firestorm.

The fires burned as long as the wind whipped them, and it wasn't until just before dark that the wind died down. Then firemen could control the last of the blazes.

Families were reunited. Slowly the shock of what had happened settled in on the people and they realized the huge loss the town had suffered. Over five thousand people were now homeless.

Most of the food had been destroyed along with the shelter and blankets. The night grew chilly then turned cold.

The fire was out, but it looked like the Cripple Creek residents would put in a cold and hungry night huddled together in any semblance of shelter they could find out of the wind.

The word spread that help was on the way. Jimmie Burns had been on the telephone before the wires burned off. He talked with the mayor of Colorado Springs, J.C. Plumb, describing the terrible fire.

People in the Springs had seen the ominous clouds rising over the mountains and knew some great tragedy had struck. Plumb had gathered the town's elite as he talked with Burns.

Stratton was there, as was Spec Penrose, Irving Howbert, and Vernor Z. Reed.

Stratton took control. He told them there was no time to raise money. "Charge everything to me and we'll worry about splitting up the bills later. We've got to move and move fast."

The committee hired a two-car special train from the Midland railroad. Wagons arrived at the Sheilds-Morley Wholesale Grocery. They loaded the wagons with cases of food and bread and took it all to the railroad station. A thousand blankets were collected from stores, and from somewhere they found 165 eight-person tents.

Someone donated a large tabernacle type tent and it all went to the depot. Even before the fire was out in Cripple Creek, the volunteers had sent relief supplies for 2,000 people to the railroad. More than fifty volunteers loaded the goods into two boxcars.

At six o'clock on Wednesday afternoon the train pulled up Ute Pass and headed for Divide. There the train was switched to the Midland Terminal tracks to run the last eighteen miles to Cripple Creek.

Just after nine o'clock that evening the train pulled into the station in Cripple Creek. Men with torches met the train and began unloading. Bert Carlton had hired two dozen freight wagons to take supplies up to the reservoir where most of the townspeople hovered.

All during the night the volunteers distributed food and supplies to the fire victims wherever they could find them.

The water system was a prime concern. That night a crew of volunteers worked at repairing any damage to get the system working again as soon as possible.

Father Volpe moved the pews in St. Peter's Church and brought in all the mothers with babies he could find.

All night organized volunteers prowled the city. Some found firewood that could be used come morning. Others organized emergency services.

Early the next morning the First National Bank of Cripple Creek opened in a half-burned warehouse. All the mines remained closed, and owners advanced paychecks to workers.

Stratton over in the Springs kept busy as well. After the first relief train left the Springs Wednesday night, he began working on outfitting a second one loaded with more supplies and food for the fire victims.

Students gathered donations of food and blankets and clothing from all around Colorado Springs. The students worked all day and men loaded the train with goods half the night. Shortly after two A.M. on Thursday, Stratton had his second relief train rolling out of the station. It arrived in Cripple Creek at dawn on Thursday.

The families of Cripple Creek responded to the tragedy. Within two days after the fire more than 3,000 of the homeless had found shelter with friends or relatives in other communities in the mining district.

Two tent cities had been erected and about 2,000 more men, women, and children were housed there. The tent cities provided two meals a day to one and all, plus a breakfast of pork chops, hot cakes, coffee, and biscuits.

Soon the mines opened and life began to edge back toward normal.

Some said that the fire was exactly what Cripple Creek needed. The buildings had been thrown up in a rush and were all wood, poorly made, and almost worthless as real estate. Now the new construction would be more studied, with a lot more brick buildings put up and with more concern about how they looked.

The building boom brought a lot of new people to town as Cripple Creek grew from 30,000 in May 1896 to almost 40,000 six months later.

Cripple Creek was back. Soon the whole town had been rebuilt, and the people returned to doing what they did best, dig gold ore out of the hills.

The fire was tragic to some and wiped out others financially, but on the whole it revitalized and energized the mining town as it had never been before. Great days still lay ahead.

CRIPPLE CREEK STARTS TO BURN. A steady wind and tinder dry, five-year-old pine wood buildings made the town a fire trap. The first fire began on a Saturday morning, on April 25, 1896. The fire died only when the wind stopped. (Photo Courtesy Pikes Peak Library District)

AFTER THE SECOND FIRE Four days after the first one, the town was virtually wiped out. Thirty acres of the heart of the town were gone, 1,500 people homeless. The people surged into rebuilding even before the ashes were cold. (Photo Courtesy Colorado Springs Pioneer Museum)

CHAPTER 16

Bob Womack's Last Days

After 1893 Bob Womack became an observer of the Cripple Creek Bonanza scene. He must have felt like a proud parent sometimes, watching the men and new money pour in, then the gold ore come out by the trainloads.

Without him there would never have been a Cripple Creek gold rush. He didn't dwell on it. For the most part, he spent his time in the Springs helping his sister Miss Lida run her boardinghouse. Their father, with them in the house, was in failing health, and both Bob and Lida felt he would die any day. Sam Womack fooled them all and lived until 1919 when he died at the age of ninety-nine years and seven months.

Bob had quit drinking after taking the "cure" and spent his time helping out in the boardinghouse, became the number two cook, and told stories with the invalids who peopled the boardinghouse at 703 North Cascade Avenue.

He had a running joke with Hiram Rogers, the Colorado Springs *Gazette* reporter who didn't run a story about Bob's gold discovery when he made it back in 1890. Bob turned into a whistler, and his tunes often reached Rogers in his office across the street from the boardinghouse.

Now and then Rogers would stick his head in the boardinghouse door, see Bob, and call to him. Rogers would ask Bob if he'd found any new Cripple Creek bonanzas. It was a standing joke between them. Bob would yell back that Rogers wouldn't put it in the paper even if he did. Then they would both have a good laugh and get back to what they were doing.

For five years, Miss Lida and Bob ran the boardinghouse. Lida had been right, there was money to be made in the business. Lots of folks from the East and even Europe were coming to the Springs to take the tuberculosis cure and needed a place to stay for six months to a year.

During this five years, Bob followed the fortunes of Cripple Creek. He nodded when friends of his struck it rich and became millionaires. He didn't envy them, but it was good to keep up with the news of the mining town. Now and again he would run into one of his old mining friends in the Springs, and they would have a cup of coffee and talk about old times. Bob was at peace and as happy as he had been in a long time.

Things were going so well in 1898 that Miss Lida reached out for larger stakes. She decided to take over the Garland Hotel. It was on the street right across from the Antlers Hotel. Some of the financing for the venture came from their old friend Theodore Lowe.

Bob's brother, William, ran the Antlers Hotel livery stable, and he began to steer tourists to the Garland. Business was good, and Lida took to the new responsibilities the way she had all her life, with a strong will and dedication. The business prospered.

Then tragedy struck, and the Antlers Hotel burned to the ground. The fire didn't spread, and the Garland was safe. Now there was added pressure on the remaining six hotels in the Springs to take care of all of the visitors, and business really roared.

After six months the pressure was as great as ever, and business kept booming. Miss Lida decided the hotel work wasn't her favorite and put the Garland up for sale. It was an ideal time to sell, and she and Bob got a lot more for it than they had paid for it.

Miss Lida took the proceeds and opened a new and much larger boardinghouse than she had before. This one was at 432 North Nevada Avenue. She also bought a smaller house on the street behind it at 121 East St. Vrain.

Bob settled into the new venture with ease, again doing kitchen work and some baking. He set up his work so he could deliver packages for a drugstore. One day Jimmie Burns met Bob with a bundle of boxes and shook his head.

Jimmie told Bob that the discoverer of Cripple Creek's Bonanza should have a nice house and people to wait on him. Jimmie Burns was a millionaire several times over by that point.

Sometime later the Springs paper came out with a story that Jimmie Burns and some of the other mine owners were going to establish a fund of $50,000 for the destitute Bob Womack so he could live comfortably for the rest of his life and not have to work at menial tasks. It was a fine story, but no such fund was ever established.

Four more years passed and Bob and Lida kept at their new boardinghouse in the Springs. Then in the spring of 1902 a letter came to Bob from the '91 club in Cripple Creek. The letter asked him to be the guest of honor at the Fourth of July celebration.

Miss Lida talked Bob into going. It was an honor for which he was long overdue. So, on July 3, Bob put on his Sunday-go-to-meeting suit. It was his black alpaca that had been in Miss Lida's cedar chest since 1899 when he went to a wedding.

He wore a striped silk shirt, gold cuff links, a high collar, and black tie. Across the black vest hung his heavy gold watch chain. A high-crowned black derby hat completed the outfit.

William Womack drove him to the Short Line railroad and sent him off. An Elks Club honor guard met him at the Cripple Creek depot and escorted him to a hotel.

The next morning the parade moved out at 10:30 with D.C. Williams as the grand marshal. The line of marchers included the police chief and his police force in its new blue uniforms. Right behind the Teller County band rolled a six-horse carriage covered with flowers and attended by top hatted coachmen.

Sitting in the grand float was Bob Womack. He sat straight and tall, smiling and waving at the crowd along Bennett Avenue. Later he said he was scared to pieces but also remarkably happy. Bob received applause as he rolled down the street. He stood now and then and doffed his derby and bowed the way he had seen famous people in parades do.

Behind him came a dozen old men, all that remained of the once great '91 Club of miners.

At the end of the parade route, Bob Womack, the man who discovered and opened the Cripple Creek Bonanza, slipped away and walked to the Short Line depot down from Warren Avenue to catch the next train to the Springs.

Back in the boardinghouse, he told Miss Lida that he enjoyed the parade, but he was sad that so many of the old-time friends had died or gone crazy or left the area.

Bob only went back to Cripple Creek once more, in July of 1904. He told Lida that he wanted to see the Poverty Gulch shack one more time. He went up on the Short Line and found the shack much the same as it had been before. He sat on the porch and remembered what it had been fifteen years before, when the whole area had two or three people.

Bob had a cold but thought nothing of it. On the trip back on the train he stared at the wonderful scenery out an open window. He propped his arm on the window ledge and enjoyed the view.

When he got to the station he realized that he couldn't move his left arm. Miss Lida came for him and the doctor said that Bob had suffered a stroke that paralyzed his left arm and affected his left leg.

Miss Lida took Bob to Pueblo for treatments in the mineral baths there, but they didn't do any good.

Old Sam Womack hadn't died as Miss Lida thought he would back in 1898. He was alive but an invalid and could barely see. Now Bob was down and couldn't move without help. This meant that now Miss Lida had two invalids to take care of. Miss Lida stopped serving meals at her boardinghouse and turned it into a rooming house so she could care for her two invalids.

Miss Lida built a bedroom on the first floor of the East St. Vrain house for Bob. There were no callers. All of the old crowd who had worked with Bob had died or moved away or were too rich to take time out for a sick call. Bob didn't complain. He lay in his bed and whiled away the days.

To help him pass the time, some of his brother's daughters came to the house to read to him. His favorite was sixteen-year-old Dorsey Womack. The pretty young girl perked up Bob every time she came. She said she loved to see Bob's face light up when she read to him.

In 1908 the local newspaper ran a series of articles about Bob, showing how his discovery of gold in Cripple Creek had benefited the Springs so much. Without the gold rush, the Springs would still be a sleepy little summer resort about one third the size it was in 1908. The story reported how most of the large buildings and firms in town were the result of Cripple Creek gold money. The editor tried to set up a retirement fund for Bob of $5,000. All he could raise in a month of articles was $800. He gave the money to Miss Lida and called off the campaign.

Bob existed day by day, not much caring if he was alive or dead. His bright spots were when Dorsey came to read to him. She read the newspaper and novels and stories. Her gentle voice always made him feel better and got him smiling.

Sometimes they just talked, and Dorsey told Bob about her boyfriends. If she asked his advice, he gave it. There was a close bonding between the two, and Bob looked forward to her daily visits.

In July 1909 Dorsey took a trip to Pueblo to visit friends. The trip turned into a series of nightly parties that left her excited and exhausted. One day Dorsey realized she had a fever, but there was a big party that night she couldn't miss.

A few days later in the middle of a game, Dorsey collapsed. The doctor said she had a bad case of typhoid fever. Ten days later she died.

Bob was devastated. Now there was nothing to brighten his day. He couldn't move without help. He lay in bed, almost always with his face to the wall. He spoke only when he had to with Miss Lida.

The first week in August, Bob lapsed into a coma. The doctor said there was nothing he could do for Bob. Both Sam, his father, and Miss Lida were with him constantly.

Bob Womack, founder of the Cripple Creek Bonanza, died quietly the evening of August 10, 1909, with his father and sister present. He was sixty-six years old.

Two days later, Bob Womack was buried next to Dorsey in the Evergreen cemetery. He was near Dorsey again; Miss Lida knew that was the way Bob would have wanted it.

It was not a large funeral. Few of his mining friends from Cripple Creek attended. There was not a miner among his pallbearers.

The man who discovered the Cripple Creek Bonanza, where thirty men became millionaires, which transformed Colorado Springs from a small town into a place three times as big and a dozen times richer, went to his rest without even a nod of acknowledgment from the booming Cripple Creek millionaire mine owners, their workers, or their families.

To his last day, Bob must have echoed his sentiments about the Cripple Creek money men that he said when he heard about Stratton becoming a millionaire. "Poor old man Stratton. All that money to worry about. . . . I don't envy him one bit."

CHAPTER 17

Bert Carlton, King of Cripple Creek

Albert E. Carlton moved to the Springs with his family in 1893. He had tuberculosis and came for the rest cure. He lost the use of one lung but recovered. His family was well-to-do, but Bert wanted to make his own way.

Many times T.B. patients were told to find an outdoor job after recovery. Bert tried his hand at driving a streetcar in the Springs, then went to a job of clerking in a department store. Neither one thrilled him.

Bert and his younger brother, Leslie, took a sightseeing trip to Cripple Creek on a lark in the fall of 1893 and found they loved the hustle and bustle, the energy of the place, the excitement of a new gold strike. They decided to stay. Their father gave each one a $10,000 stake to get started in some business.

ALBERT E. CARLTON went to Cripple Creek with $10,000 from his wealthy father and instructions to make his fortune. He did. Bert Carlton and his brother started a coal and firewood business, and before he was done he owned most of the producing mines in Cripple Creek and made millions. (Photo Courtesy Pikes Peak Library District)

They opened a coal and firewood business. It began small with Bert as the salesman and Leslie delivering the products on a burro with pack racks.

Bert had been introduced to the mining business in Cripple Creek when Winfield Scott Stratton offered to sell him a half interest in the Independence mine for $500 two years earlier. Later Bert wished that he had made the deal.

When the railroads began their march toward Cripple Creek, Bert looked over both the lines and even before they arrived decided that the Midland Terminal would be the winner in the battle for ore. But the railroad couldn't run past each mine.

He met with Collbran and suggested a deal. He and his brother were starting a wagon hauling business to transport ore from the mines to the railroads.

Bert asked Collbran: If his transfer company guaranteed to bring a lot of ore to Collbran's railroad when it arrived, would he give Bert's company a monopoly on delivering to the railroad customers all of the freight that came in on the train?

Bert was then twenty-six or twenty-seven. The railroad man told Bert he had nothing to lose at that point. He said his road would not be to Cripple Creek for a while, but when it arrived, Bert had his deal.

Bert and his brother set up the Colorado Trading and Transfer Company at Bennett and Fifth streets. Bert and Leslie began generating hauling business, and when the Midland Terminal rails arrived in Midland, they were ready. They had sold several mine owners on the idea of letting them do the short haul job of getting their ore to the railroad's ore cars at Midland for the shorter trip to the Springs than the Florence & Cripple Creek offered.

Bert was off and running. His next deal was to get exclusive rights to distribute coal in Cripple Creek from the Pueblo-based Colorado Fuel and Iron Company. Wood had been used for fuel, but as timber grew scarcer on the surrounding hills, coal came in to use, first in the coal-fired steam hoists in the mines. Then later when water threatened the mines, they installed coal-fired steam pumps to keep the water levels down.

Business boomed. The miners relied on Bert to supply them with coal so they could keep mining. The railroad loved his ability to get ore to the tracks from mines without sidings. More wagons, more customers, more drivers, then more wagons.

In 1898 Bert bought the First National Bank of Cripple Creek from partners J. Lindsay and Jim Parker. In 1899 Bert made a secret deal with Midland Terminal to sell his wagon transfer company to them.

Bert was six feet tall, slender, with ulcers, and unmarried. At least Cripple Creek thought he was unmarried. Actually he had secretly married a girl back in Illinois when he visited his old hometown. They decided to keep it a secret until he was over his tuberculosis and had made a half million dollars.

Now he had made his half million and had let his mother push him into an engagement with a girl there in the Springs. He was married and was engaged to another woman. Before it all worked out he had asked still another woman to marry him.

Eventually he divorced his child bride, got unengaged from one girl, and married his lady love.

What was next? In Cripple Creek, Bert worked in the Republican party but stayed in the background. His offices and apartment over the bank became an unofficial center for financial strategy with mine owners and political maneuvering. Bert knew all of the mine owners' secrets from his banking ties, and now he put that knowledge to use.

He bought several mines at bargain prices, such as the Doctor Jack Pot and the Findley. Both were rich in ore. The Jack Pot produced $7.5 million over its lifetime and the Findley had gold taken out worth over $3 million.

Bert knew the mining community so well that he kept his eye out for apex problems. Whenever he found an apex situation where the gold vein did not surface on the owner's claim, he launched a lawsuit. Apex suits were hard to defend against and usually lengthy and could tie up a mine operation, so many of those sued simply settled.

Bert kept expanding his numbers of mines and property. He watched the other mine owners and those amassing huge numbers of mines and claims. Bert kept on the alert to protect what he had built up.

Bert was aware of possible competition to his transfer operation back in 1897 when L.D. Ross, a real estate man from the Springs, built the High Line, an electric railway for passengers. It was six miles long and ran from Cripple Creek up the hills to Hoosier Pass. There it turned south around Bull Hill past Windy Point and on down Battle Mountain into Victor. The High Line was for passengers only, but Bert worried that it could be converted to freight service or ore hauling.

The High Line was successful, so Ross decided to put in the Low Line. This one went from Victor to the north. In 1899 Ross had his Low Line extended through Goldfield and to Independence. That same year Ross sold his two electric lines to a group of miners headed by Stratton and Jimmie Burns, who said they also planned to build a new railroad on a direct route to Colorado Springs.

The standard gauge electric line would be used for picking up ore at the mines. A new transfer company would be formed. A new mill would be built by the group for processing their gold in the Springs.

They called it the Short Line, and with Stratton and Jimmie Burns behind the plan, they lined up a lot of the mine owners to support them.

The Short Line started with $3.5 million for construction, and the builders could get whatever more they needed. The mine owners put in a first-class road and equipped it with the best in cars, engines, furnishings, and comfort.

Bert and the Midland Terminal knew they were in a war, and one that would be hard to win. Bert pressured every gold mine owner who owed him money or who ever had owed him or his bank money to stay with M-T for its gold ore shipments.

The Midland Terminal line cut freight rates and built spur lines into any gold mine that was shipping a wagonload a week.

The Short Line was picturesque, closer to the Springs, and had the latest and best equipment, but it lost the war to Midland Terminal. The new railroad had amateurs running it. The hardened longtime professional train men on the Midland Terminal simply outdid them, beat them to the punch, and won the war.

Jimmie Burns and Irving Howbert sold the line in 1905 to Colorado and Southern who promptly leased it to the Midland Terminal.

As soon as one crisis ended for Bert Carlton, another one seemed to loom on the horizon.

The Cripple Creek Mining District had been without any labor trouble since the first strike ended in 1894. Since that time the mines grew richer, and the labor union grew stronger. Soon the Western Federation of Miners developed into the strongest industrial union in the country. Headquarters were in Denver, and in 1902 Charles Moyer became its president.

In those days the real power of the union was the executive secretary, Big Bill Haywood. Big Bill was a socialist and hated mine owners more than anything on earth.

He decided to confront the mine owners in Cripple Creek because the district had the most W.F.M. members anywhere in the country. He began by pushing through a rule in the locals that the local officers could take action without a vote of the membership. He instructed the miners what newspapers to read, made out scab worker lists, and wined and dined the Teller County officials to stay on good terms with them.

In the Springs, he unionized the mill workers. The Standard Mill workers signed up. In August Haywood called the mill men out on strike. To make sure he shut down the mill, he called out the 3,500 gold miners in the Cripple Creek District, closing fifty mines.

Bert went to war again.

He called a meeting of the mine owners' association, and they revitalized and strengthened it. They issued work permits to all miners who would quit the W.F.M. and go to work. Within days, Bert had helped open ten mines with nonunion labor.

The union responded with random violence and acts of terror. This brought the state militia and a confrontation. Some miners were jailed, then released, and more violence shook the district.

By November things were no better. More union men turned in their union cards and went into the nonunion mines. More violence came then and culminated in a bomb explosion on the sixth level of the Vindicator mine that killed two supervisors.

That brought back the militia, and the Cripple Creek Mining District went under martial law. It was tough. General Bell locked up local police, packed the Goldfield bull pen with union men, and even intimidated the courts.

Then the break came. One of the men who blew up a train confessed to General Bell that he did it on orders from union officers and that they were instructed by Haywood. Sentiment shifted to the nonunion side. More and more miners deserted the W.F.M. and went into the mines. More mines opened. Violence stopped and the miners' union went into hiding.

Chapter 17

The first week in February 1904, Governor Peabody ended the martial law and most of the troops went home. Things settled down but the strike was still on.

At the W.F.M. that summer, Big Bill Hayward got challenged and almost fired for spending almost a half million dollars on the Cripple Creek strike that had accomplished little. One of his supporters was determined to get the strike back on course. He decided to kill some more people in the Cripple Creek District and get the militia back, and then popular opinion would swing back to the strikers.

Harry Orchard was the bomber who took on the task. He wound up in Independence with two cases of dynamite and a man to help him, Steve Adams. They prepared the dynamite with a simple wooden tilt-up trigger that would spill acid on giant caps, setting them off and detonating the dynamite.

The night of June 5, when Independence was sleeping, they carried the dynamite to the Florence and Cripple Creek railroad depot. They hid the dynamite on the ground under the depot platform and put the giant caps on the sticks of dynamite. Orchard took out the corks on the bottles of acid and placed them on the special tilt-up assembly so they could be tilted and emptied on the caps.

Orchard stretched a wire from the tilt-ups across the tracks and tied the wire to an old chair leg. The two men waited in the shadows for the train. One was scheduled for 2:15 A.M. to bring in a nonunion crew for the graveyard shift on Bert Carlton's Findley mine.

Miners coming off the night shift collected on the platform waiting for the train to take them home. Soon the platform was crowded with nonunion miners.

A minute later, the train came around a curve and approached the depot. The platform was overflowing with men now. When the train was less than a hundred yards from the depot, Orchard and Adams stood up and pulled the wire, tilting the acid.

Two thunderous explosions rocked the scene, and a pair of daylight-like flashes filled the sky. Thirteen men on the platform were killed instantly and another fourteen suffered injuries. Parts of bodies were blown 150 feet from the station.

The train coming in was undamaged and no one on it was injured. At daylight Bert Carlton was there along with the sheriff and doctors and nurses. Six of the injured had amputations later to save their lives.

The nonunion mines did not work that Monday morning. The bombers got away by soaking their shoes in turpentine to leave no trace for bloodhounds. They both escaped to the Springs and then went to Denver and on to Wyoming. Neither man was ever caught or punished for the mass murder.

The militia came again, and 225 W.F.M. members were summarily arrested and deported across the state lines into Kansas and New Mexico. The bombing drove out the union from Cripple Creek and all of Colorado. Big Bill Haywood went on to be one of the founders of the radical I.W.W. union and waged war against the United States for fifteen more years.

Bert Carlton settled in to consolidate his investments. He was still important in the district, but he was not immensely wealthy the way Stratton had been. He could fight off small challenges but couldn't take on the heavyweights like John T. Milliken. The small-statured man was a driving force in the district after 1900. He bought mines and built a reduction mill. In 1908 he bought the United Gold Mine Company, a huge consolidation of more than a hundred Cripple Creek District mines. He was a big player in the game.

HEARSES BEAR THE BODIES OF fifteen miners killed at the Independence mine train platform where they waited to go home after a shift. A striker blew up the platform just as the train came in. It was the largest group of casualties in the strike. All twenty-seven men on the platform were killed or seriously wounded. (Photo Courtesy Pikes Peak Library District)

For a time, Bert wondered if he would be squeezed out of Cripple Creek. He figured that the area wasn't big enough for two big punchers like himself and Milliken. The trouble was, Milliken had hundreds of millions to play with. Bert was much more limited than that.

Then Bert called in his old friends who had gone to Utah and become multimillionaires in their copper mines. Spec Penrose and Charlie MacNeill had the money; they looked over the holdings and the potential and decided to back Bert in his plans. It was 1910 and the partners had been in the copper mines for six years. MacNeill had a monthly income of $100,000, and Penrose earned twice that much with more stock. The men joked that they could buy the whole state of Colorado if they wanted to.

Bert began his sales efforts. He pointed out to Penrose that the Roosevelt tunnel would open up many of the flooded mines to further operation. Bert said if he ran the principal mines, many now owned by Milliken, and the mill and the railroad, they could clean up.

It would mean that since the mines were connected underground, much of the hoisting machinery could be idled. They would stabilize stock prices and produce as much ore as the mill needed to run at optimum capacity.

It was a bold plan and Penrose and MacNeill liked it. Bert began pressuring Milliken at every opportunity. It turned into a corporation battle, since Bert and Milliken owned lots of stock in each other's corporations.

Stock deals, board member wrangles, director meetings, and complicated stock and legal moves all followed once Bert began to shoot for Milliken's holdings.

Bert was winning the small battles, but the betting around town was that Milliken had too much fire power for the hometown boy, Bert Carlton. The betting crowd didn't know about Bert's deal with the copper kings for backing.

The slugfest continued for over four years, and Bert kept on winning points in the battle, but it was far from over.

Then in late 1914 Milliken suddenly gave up. He was not in the best position on many areas and issues, and he had found a real black bonanza in Oklahoma oil that would take all of his time. He began to deal with Bert.

In late February the first deal was announced. Milliken separated the Golden Cycle mine at Cripple Creek from the mill at Colorado City, and the mine sold to the Vindicator for $1.5 million.

The next big deal to rock the district was when Milliken sold the Golden Cycle Mill in Colorado City for $4.5 million to Bert, Spencer Penrose, and Eugene Shove. This deal included the United Gold Mines (100 of them), the lignite coal mines, $500,000 in cash and the $1.5 million that Bert had just paid to Milliken for the Golden Cycle mine.

With all the Milliken interests out of the way, Bert had an open field to consolidate the mining and mill operations and control Cripple Creek.

One flaw was the rich Cresson mine. Bert asked them to name a price and they did: $3.9 million. Bert put together a syndicate of eight money men, including one financier from Denver, and bought the mine.

Now Bert had almost all of Cripple Creek's major producing mines and the big processing mill.

Later he bought back his Colorado Trading and Transfer Company and the Midland Terminal railroad and then its connecting line, the Colorado Midland.

When 1930 arrived Bert Carlton owned mines in the Cripple Creek District that had produced $227 million in gold. He owned all of the major mines except the Portland and the Strong.

By 1915 Bert had moved with his wife Ethel to a new home in Colorado Springs on millionaire's row. He had lived in his apartment over the bank all these years and put in twenty-two years in the gold camp before he moved out.

Bert had amassed a fortune that not even he would have imagined when he went up to Cripple Creek to "see what was going on" and decided to stay. He lived much of his last year in an apartment in the Broadmoor Hotel in the Springs.

His wife began building a big new home for them north of Colorado Springs in Pine Valley, but Bert couldn't get excited about it. When it was partly finished, Ethel drove Bert out to look at the place. He took sick there and died a few days later of uremic poisoning. Bert was sixty-five years old.

After his death, his brother Leslie took over control of the corporations and ran them much the way he thought

Bert would have done. Leslie died seven years later, and Ethel took over and managed the companies.

Bob Womack discovered the Cripple Creek Bonanza, Winfield Scott Stratton pushed it into greatness, and then along came Bert Carlton, who hitched the whole district to a star and pushed it to its pinnacle as the greatest gold camp.

CHAPTER 18

Tunnel Time in Cripple Creek

In placer mining, water is a vital element. In deep hard rock mines, water can be the operation's worst enemy—and it can close down a bonanza.

Cripple Creek had its share and then some of water problems. Most of the district is situated in an old volcano cauldron. The top of the land mass there is about 10,000 feet on average. The sides of the cauldron, made of tough-as-steel granite walls, extend upward to an average height of 9,200 feet. The granite forms a huge cup that traps rain water and snow runoff.

There is no outlet of springs or streams below the 9,200-foot level. A problem for miners? A huge one.

With a start at 10,000 feet, the hard rock miners could work down only 800 feet with their shafts before they ran into water. It was the kind of water that didn't just seep in, it lived there and stayed there.

The only way the hard rock men could penetrate below 800 feet was to install pumps and lift the water out the top of the shaft and let it run down the mountain.

Miners had been doing this for ten years. The coal-fired pumps were costly to run and expensive to buy, but in the short haul there was no other way.

Bert Carlton thought there was a better way. His solution was to dig a drainage tunnel straight out from the mine to the edge of the mountain and penetrate that granite wall that was trapping all of the water.

Bert helped drill several small drainage tunnels that punched through the side of the cauldron wall and let out the water. But most of them were too small, too short, and served only a few mines.

Bert pushed for a larger tunnel, the El Paso, that was completed in 1904 and cost $80,000. It breached the cauldron's granite wall at the 8,800-foot level. It was a little over 5,700 feet long and drained the Doctor Jack Pot and some other mines. The tunnel spewed water out of its opening about three miles below the town of Cripple Creek into the town's namesake stream, where it was of no concern to the miners.

It worked, but Bert said it wasn't big enough or long enough to solve the water problem. He wanted a $500,000 tunnel to drain most of the mines in the cauldron.

The other mine owners who had all contributed to the El Paso tunnel told Bert he was crazy. Mining went on with the use of the big pumps. Bert still wanted to build a larger tunnel.

In 1906 a lot of water poured into the cauldron from heavy rains and snows. In March a deluge of water broke through into the tunnels of the El Paso below the fourth level and the water rose rapidly.

The El Paso drain tunnel was simply too small to handle that quantity of water, and water rushed into the El Paso tunnels and up shafts at the rate of 5,000 gallons a minute. Before Bert could get his pumps out of the mine, the water rose 600 feet. Bert lost $40,000 worth of pumps in an hour. In the near panic that followed, the El Paso stock value slumped by a total of half a million dollars. Stocks in other mines around Beacon hill plummeted as well.

Bert screamed at the other mine owners that he had been right, they should have dug a huge drainage tunnel. He estimated that the mine owners would lose at least $5 million before the water could be pumped out of the mines and the massive damage reversed.

With Bert on their backs night and day, the mine owners at last decided to build a larger drain tunnel.

They talked and planned and argued, and it wasn't until March of 1907 that they hired a contractor to do the job. They put $400,000 in the bank to finance the project. They called it the Roosevelt Deep Drainage Tunnel. The contractor said he could do the job in two years, ten feet a day, at a cost of twenty-one dollars a foot.

Work began on May Day of 1907 at Gatch Park down the Cripple Creek's stream bed. The granite wall was tougher than the drillers thought. After eight months they were only half as far as they should have been, which meant the project could cost over $800,000. Some of the mine owners wanted to cancel the whole project. Bert Carlton saved the day . . . again. He proved to them that if the tunnel didn't puncture the bowl at the 8,000-foot level, all the mines would be flooded in three years and production stopped. He told them there was still over $300 million worth of gold in the mines waiting to be mined—if the tunnel went through.

When he had them convinced, Bert said he could do the drilling himself at eight feet a day for twenty-eight dollars a foot. They at last agreed and signed a contract. Bert picked out his men. Most had no experience drilling drainage tunnels. But Bert knew his men.

Bert began drilling on February 1, 1908. It took him nearly three years, but he finished the tunnel in 1910. It ran for 15,737 feet. The nearly three miles of tunnel drained the mines down to the 8,000-foot level, meaning they could sink shafts down to an average of 2,000 feet from the surface instead of only 800 feet of "dry tunnels."

Of the top-producing mines, five of them went to the 2,000-foot level or below. The Portland went to 3,200 feet and the Cresson bored to 2,400 feet. All of the big bonanza mines were well below the original 800-foot dry level working limit.

The first three miles of the tunnel cost $530,000, the best money the mine owners ever spent. It disgorged 8,500 gallons of water a minute.

Later the Roosevelt tunnel was extended up to 4.6 miles to serve other areas of the district. Without that first three miles of tunnel by Bert Carlton, the mines of Cripple Creek would never have achieved the massive totals of gold production that they did.

The effects of the tunnel were soon felt. Water had been at the level of the old El Paso tunnel at 8,800 feet. Now the water began draining down at the rate of 110 feet a year.

That meant that whole new areas were opened to mining in the rich Portland, Vindicator, El Paso, Granite, Elkton, Gold Dollar, and many other of the long-established mines. Cripple Creek began to roar again.

The Roosevelt tunnel served the area well until the late 1930s when water again became a problem. By that time Ethel Carlton ran the corporation. She owned most of the mines and decided that a new tunnel was needed to keep up production and to open new areas.

Her plan was to drill a new tunnel over 1,100 feet below the Roosevelt Tunnel. She got her way. The new drainage bore was called the Carlton Tunnel and was over six miles long. In 1941 the new tunnel was finished, and it drained the mines down to the 6,900-foot level. Now most of the mines could work down 3,100 feet without the use of heavy water pumps.

Ethel must have smiled when the tunnel was finished. She knew that this was what Bert would have done to keep the mines at Cripple Creek producing.

PRACTICE, PRACTICE, PRACTICE. These miners do their practice training for the Fourth of July hole drilling contest to be held in 1897. The challenge was to see how quickly a man could sink a three-foot hole in a granite boulder with a steel star drill and an eight-pound hammer. It was a popular contest. (Photo Courtesy Pikes Peak Library District)

CHAPTER 19

The Cresson and its Vug

The old gambling truism is that you've got to know when to hold 'em and when to fold 'em.

Two insurance men from Chicago just didn't know when to give up when it came to a "barren" Cripple Creek gold claim. They were brothers, J.R. and Eugene Harbeck, and some say that they went on a drinking bout one night in the lesser regions of Chicago, and when they sobered up the next morning they had bought a hole in the ground in Cripple Creek called the Cresson claim.

Not a mine yet, just a hole in the ground with no gold in it and a lot of money needed to develop it if there were any gold ore down there. That was back in 1894. The brothers didn't have enough money to work the claim right to see if it had any gold.

Everyone around Cripple Creek had given up on it and called it an empty hole. But the brothers held on. When good news came from Cripple Creek about the gold mining in the newspapers, the brothers sold some shares of their stock to the uninitiated in Chicago and hurried to Cripple Creek to do some more digging.

The locals they hired to work were pleased, but privately they knew it was a barren hole in the ground.

Old-timers around Cripple Creek chuckled about the work the brothers were doing. They said the mine wasn't even in a good spot. The Cresson was above the Elkton mine in a barren little gulch between Bull Hill and Raven Hill. The saloon talk was that the only thing the brothers would find in the Cresson was water, and then only if they dug deep enough.

In gold mining there is a process known as leasing. A mine owner or claim owner gives a man or company a lease with the right to dig in that hole for a specific time. He provides all of his own tools and equipment and manpower and pays all of his expenses.

One of the lessors over the years on the Cresson claim was Frank Ish, who at one time owned the *Cripple Creek Crusher* newspaper. Ish put considerable money and effort into the Cresson. He sank a shaft 600 feet deep and put out many drifts and tunnels but went broke and left town. He didn't find a shovel full of gold ore.

The spot where the Cresson was situated in the gully was so steep and narrow that the railroad refused to put in a spur line. There was no need anyway since the mine hadn't produced. In the long run, the brothers Harbecks spent a lot of money just getting to and from their mine with equipment and supplies.

The man who managed the digging on the Cresson for the owners quit, and the Harbecks asked the hottest mining man in town, Bert Carlton, to find them a new manager. He did, a small, stocky man in his mid-thirties by the name of Dick Roelofs. He was no hotshot, but if Carlton said he could do the job, the Harbecks went along with him.

No one knows for sure, but the word around Cripple Creek was that the Harbecks had run up a debt of $80,000, and all they had to show for it was a new manager and a 600-foot hole.

Roelofs picked up Luke Shepherd as his foreman and a small crew and they went to work. From that first day on, Roelofs didn't say a word about the progress on the Cresson. It was a news blackout that held tight.

Word soon leaked out that Roelofs had hit a huge strike of low-grade ore, maybe fifteen dollars a ton, and was making it pay by using new mining techniques and brilliant management. Everyone knew that he used the pillar system. This involved driving lateral tunnels every twenty feet from the main drift. When he hit pay dirt, he did stoping that left "rooms" big enough to fit the Palace Hotel into.

Slowly people realized that Roelofs was onto something. He invented new ways to do the mining. He solved the ore loading problem by erecting an aerial tram from the Cresson's lift house a mile down the gulch to the Elkton mill, where there was a spur line of the railroad.

Word got out that Roelofs had produced $60,000 worth of gold during the year 1910. Nobody knew for sure, because the brothers Harbeck didn't make public their earning statements. The gossips figured that during 1911 the Cresson paid out $100,000 in gold and in 1912 up to $150,000.

The Cresson remained much a mystery during the year 1913 and 1914, but people in Cripple Creek figured they must be making money in that "dud" of a hole. Then Harbecks hired a well-known mining tax expert and lawyer from the Springs named Hildreth Frost. You don't need a tax lawyer if you're not making money, Cripple Creek wags decided.

The Cresson made history on November 24, 1914, when lawyer Frost answered his phone in the Springs. Dick

Roelofs was on the other end, and Roelofs asked Frost if he was alone. When Frost said he was, Roelofs told him that he wanted him to drop whatever he was doing and take the night train to Cripple Creek. Roelofs said not to tell anyone he was going and to go directly to his rooms on the corner of Bennett and Second as soon as he arrived. Roelofs urged Frost to get to Cripple Creek as quickly as he could.

Frost did as Dick requested.

It was after ten that night of November 24 when Frost climbed the stairs to Dick Roelofs' rooms.

Frost banged on the door but got no answer. Frost knocked again and called out his name through the door. The door unlocked and edged out. The miner pulled the door open, jerked Frost inside, shut the door quickly, and locked it.

Roelofs pulled up a chair and talked in a whisper. He told Frost that in the afternoon something happened in the mine that was so tremendous, so big and important, that he needed witnesses. It was on the twelfth level in the mine, and Roelofs said he needed Frost and another witness to go in there with him. He said he wanted Frost to get Ed De La Vergne to be the other witness.

Frost knew that Roelofs had been a miracle worker in the dud of a Cresson mine and made it pay. He had to go along with whatever Roelofs wanted. He called Ed at Elkton and made the date for first thing the next morning.

On November 25, 1914, Roelofs and Frost rode the Low Line electric railroad to Elkton. They met Ed and the three walked the mile up the canyon road to the Cresson shaft house where the foreman gave them magnesium flares.

Dick wouldn't say a word about what they were going to look at. The questions came quickly, then trailed off when the questions were not answered.

At the twelfth level of the Cresson mine, Dick walked the two around for twenty minutes so they didn't know where they were in the maze of tunnels and drifts and connecting tunnels. Then he turned off a drift into a lateral and stopped in front of a double steel door at the end of the lateral.

Roelofs picked up a drill and slammed it three times against the steel door, and it slowly opened from the inside. Behind the door stood three men each with two revolvers in their hands ready to shoot. They saw Roelofs and relaxed.

The mine manager walked forward. Behind the guards on the floor of the lateral was a platform three feet high and five feet wide with a ladder up it. In the lateral wall in front of the platform was a cut five feet wide. Roelofs stepped up on the platform next to the dark opening in the wall and motioned for the other two to come up with him. Then Dick took a match and lit one of the magnesium flares and pushed it through the five-foot-wide hole into what had been coal-black darkness.

What they saw was a glittering jewel box filled with sparkling gems of great price. They saw a cave that was twenty feet long, fifteen feet wide, and nearly forty feet high, a huge treasure room filled with millions of gold crystals. They were sylvanite and calaverite. Among the crystals were more millions of flakes of gold a half-inch across.

The crystals on the floor showed in humps and lumps with piles of white quartz sand.

The magnesium flare sputtered out and Dick lit a second one as the men feasted on the dream of every gold miner who ever carried a pick.

When the second flare faded, they moved back to the lateral and Dick explained it to Frost.

It was a giant geode. That was what the geologists called it. It was a hollow, rounded nodule of rock lined with gold crystals or other formations. Most geodes could be held in one hand. This was simply a gigantic one. In mining it was called a "vug."

Ed had seen one once about four feet long and half that high. It was nothing like this. He offered Roelofs his congratulations.

Roelofs asked Ed how much the vug would produce. Ed guessed that the crystals in the wall showing would be worth a hundred thousand dollars.

Roelofs reposted the guards, and the three men left the mine. Dick wired the owners that he had made a great find and suggested they come down and take a look. He didn't tell them exactly what it was.

Then he began mining. No ore cars for this one. They scraped off the crystals and put them in gunny sacks and guarded them on the way to the mill.

Dick's crew dug out 1,400 sacks of the crystals and they paid out a total of $378,000. Then they went in and took out another 1,000 sacks of lower-grade ore that yielded another $91,000. Next the walls of the vug were mined back several yards and produced another $700,000 in pure gold.

The Cresson vug had produced $1.2 million in gold in four weeks of work. The profit percentage must have been well over 95 percent.

The Harbecks were not stingy with their newfound wealth. They declared a $200,000 dividend, and after Christmas the "suckers" who had bought stock in a "dud" mine took in another $1 million in dividends. That meant that each of those investors in Chicago, who had bought those "sucker" shares of the Cresson mine some ten to fifteen years ago, had received more than ten times their original investment.

Dick Roelofs became an instant celebrity, and his name was known around the gold mining world. Three years after the find, he retired, became a big stockholder in the Cresson, and went to New York City to live in luxury as a fashionable man about town, determined to have his share of expensive fun. He enjoyed the next thirty years of his life in the big city.

The Cresson mine, the late bloomer that was called a dud for so many years, wound up as the second largest producer of gold in the district right behind the Portland. The Cresson miners dug out $49 million in gold.

Never say never to a gold miner.

CHAPTER 20

The Years Since

The Carlton Tunnel that drained Cripple Creek mines down to 6,900 feet above sea level was completed in 1941. Almost before it had a chance to benefit the miners, the war broke out.

Orders came down from the government quickly. Gold mining was not considered essential to the war effort; therefore the mines were to be virtually closed down. The miners involved would be switched to coal mining, copper mining, and other minerals that were vital to building a huge war machine, defending our shores, and furthering the war effort generally.

So, most of the mines were closed. A few still operated, but producing mines went from 105 in 1940 down to 22 in 1943 and to 19 in 1945. Production slumped to $999,000 in gold shipped during the last year of the war.

After the war, many of the mines opened again. Inflation had lifted the cost of working them to a point where it was much harder to make a profit with gold at thirty-five dollars an ounce. Something had to change.

In 1949 Ethel Carlton still ran the Carlton empire and had a stranglehold on the mines in Cripple Creek. She had an idea. She knew that the overhead had to be slashed or new ways of mining found.

She began by dismantling the Midland Terminal Railroad and the Golden Cycle Mill in Colorado City in 1949. The cost of hauling the ore that far was not practical.

To replace the mill, she put up a new one at Cripple Creek. The site she chose was just below the Elkton and Cresson mines. It was the Carlton Cyanide Mill and cost $2 million. This mill could treat ore at a cost of about three dollars a ton. If the gold ore was worth only five or six or seven dollars a ton, the miners and the mill owner could still make money. The new mill was up and operating in 1951.

The new mill brought a resurgence of mining in Cripple Creek through the 1950s and the 1960s but good ore was getting harder and harder to find.

TOP PRODUCING MINES IN CRIPPLE CREEK

Through the good years of Cripple Creek some of the mines set record production. Here is a list of those and their total gold value production and their deepest penetration into the bowels of the Cripple Creek cauldron:

Mine	Production	Depth in Feet
Portland	$60,000,000	3,200
Cresson	49,000,000	2,400
Independence	28,000,000	1,420
Vindicator	27,200,000	2,150
Golden Cycle	22,510,000	2,170
Ajax	20,700,000	2,600
Elkton	16,200,000	1,700

Mine	Production	Depth in Feet
Granite	15,828,000	1,000
Isabella Group	15,700,000	1,150
Strong	13,000,000	950
El Paso Beacon Hill	10,800,000	1,300
Mary McKinney	10,700,000	1,400
Last Dollar	7,500,000	1,600
Dr. Jack Pot	7,126,000	1,000
Hull City	5,010,000	1,200
Jerry Johnson	5,000,000	900
Findley	3,137,000	1,400
Anchoria Leland	3,000,000	1,300
Gold King. .Womack's El Paso	3,000,000	1,000

GOLD PRODUCTION CRIPPLE CREEK DISTRICT

Just how much gold was produced in the district during the early years, through the boom times, and into the decline? These records from the U.S. Bureau of Mines show these totals up to 1962.

Year	Gold Produced	Working Mines	Year	Gold Produced	Working Mines
1890	0	0	1920	4,360,960	41
1891	$ 200,000	3	1921	4,329,218	47
1892	557,841	50	1922	4,062,044	55
1893	2,025,518	150	1923	4,065,545	48
1894	2,634,349	175	1924	4,960,716	43
1895	6,210,622	250	1925	4,608,604	40
1896	7,456,763	350	1926	4,451,992	36
1897	10,167,782	400	1927	3,321,875	50
1898	13,547,350	450	1928	3,070,203	49
1899	16,107,943	475	1929	2,644,961	41
1900	18,199,736	475	1930	2,535,378	63
1901	17,288,030	475	1931	2,385,769	41
1902	16,965,689	475	1932	2,200,724	52
1903	11,862,739	325	1933	2,273,878	111
1904	14,484,270	225	1934	4,479,966	135
1905	15,676,494	200	1935	4,300,891	130
1906	13,976,727	160	1936	4,956,287	135
1907	10,404,360	155	1937	5,089,899	136
1908	13,059,620	150	1938	5,092,556	134
1909	11,499,093	150	1939	4,702,125	110
1910	11,031,555	145	1940	4,533,831	105
1911	10,593,278	145	1941	4,686,810	99
1912	11,049,024	144	1942	3,667,061	42
1913	10,948,008	140	1943	1,584,039	22
1914	12,045,364	140	1944	1,084,289	20
1915	13,727,992	140	1945	999,049	19
1916	12,172,061	140	1946	1,673,489	25
1917	10,448,051	135	1947	2,041,738	37
1918	8,170,412	75	1948	1,874,915	28
1919	5,867,511	41	1949	473,805	13

Year	Gold Produced	Working Mines	Year	Gold Produced	Working Mines
1950	No Bureau of Mines Record		1957	1,644,845	
1951	No Bureau of Mines Record		1958	1,501,005	
1952	1,698,445		1959	993,193	
1953	1,804,565		1960	1,100,000	
1954	No Record		1961	922,048	
1955	495,985		1962	451,803	
1956	1,839,040				

1963 to 1975. . . .No record with U.S. Bureau of Mines annual Mineral Yearbooks of any Teller County gold production.

The Carlton mill closed down at the end of 1961, and that ended any large-scale mining in the Cripple Creek District for the next fourteen years. As the average price of gold began to rise in 1971, the mine operators looked at their properties again.

The Golden Cycle began to investigate its mines. In 1971 the United States government raised the official price of gold from thirty-five dollars to thirty-eight dollars. By 1971 the price of gold was up to $41.25 on average. The next year it went to $58.60 and then in 1973 the average price of gold during the year zoomed to $97.81. By 1975 the average market price of gold was up to $161.49.

Work was now under way to reestablish gold mining in the Cripple Creek District, including reprocessing of over 400 acres of tailings from the Carlton mill in Colorado Springs.

After the U. S. government let gold float on a free market in 1974, there was another upsurge of mining in Cripple Creek. But by then most of the rich deposits had been cleaned out over the twenty-five years since the 1950s.

Trying to compare the dollar amount of gold taken out of Cripple Creek after 1974 with that mined previously is like judging apples against grapefruit. When gold floated on the free market at or near the international price, it was much higher than the official price of thirty-five dollars an ounce that had been in effect since 1933.

A thousand ounces of gold mined in 1960 would be worth $35,000. The same thousand ounces of gold mined after 1975 would be worth whatever the market value was for gold on that particular day that the gold was sold.

The price of gold has varied all over the scale since it went into the free market. In 1995 the price was still up and down but often around $400 an ounce. Which means that same 1,000 ounces of gold sold today would bring not the $35,000 it did in 1960, but $400,000. That's why you can't judge the value of gold taken from Cripple Creek after 1974 with the dollar amounts taken prior to that time.

CRIPPLE CREEK AT ZENITH in 1901 looked like this. The picture was taken by Julia Skolas who had a photo studio in town at 222 South Tijon Street from 1899 to 1901. The original broad streets as platted by the founders still show. (Photo Courtesy Pikes Peak Library District)

CHAPTER 21

Cripple Creek Today

Yes, they're still mining gold at Cripple Creek.

Today gold mining is still taking place in Cripple Creek, however it's slightly different from the early days. Today's mining is done in open-pit fashion. Gold bearing ore is not dug and transported by shovel and ore cart, but by thirteen-ton front loaders and eighty-five-ton dump trucks.

No high grading here. The average gold content of the ore is between 0.03 hundredths of an ounce a ton and 0.036 hundredths of an ounce per ton. The company doing the mining says that this extremely low level of gold in the ore is still an economically feasible operation.

Who is doing this mammoth scale open pit gold mining?

The company is the Cripple Creek and Victor Gold Mining Company, which has been in operation in the Cripple Creek Mining District since 1982.

The company has taken advantage of new technology and higher gold prices to recover gold from disseminated deposits and with large-scale surface mining techniques. In the 1980s the CC&V company reprocessed historic "waste" rock taken from the underground mines and thrown away.

From September of 1989 through 1993 the company discovered mineable deposits in the near-surface part of the volcanic caldera around the historic Cresson underground mine. More studies showed that mining this surface area was feasible, and processing of the ore could be done in a leach facility located nearby.

This operation is a joint venture between the Pikes Peak Mining Company and Golden Cycle Gold Corporation. Pikes Peak Mining Company is the managing agent for the joint venture.

To get the low grade, near surface ore, the company uses conventional surface, open pit mining methods. This involves clearing, drilling, blasting, loading, and hauling the ore by truck. Engineering estimates put the probable reserves of ore at the Cresson mine surface area that will produce 0.036 ounces of gold per ton, at more than forty-eight million tons.

A crushing facility immediately to the south of the mine will reduce the ore to less than 1.5 inches and it will be sent by overland conveyor over Highway 67 to a loadout bin adjacent to the valley leach facility just below the Arequa Gulch.

The area to be mined includes about 190 acres around the old Cresson mine.

The leach facility is where the ore winds up and is designed to contain forty-eight million tons of ore. The facility has a triple liner system to prevent any of the solutions from escaping. The sodium cyanide system is used to separate the gold from other metals in the ore. Cyanide milling of Cripple Creek gold ore was used almost from the start and has been used in various mills in the area ever since.

The crushed ore is stacked on a leach pad. Impermeable plastic membranes line the area on which the rock is placed. Next a sodium cyanide solution is dripped on the crushed ore, dissolving, or leaching, the gold particles from it.

A solution which now contains the gold is collected and processed. This filters out the gold from the rock, and the reusable sodium cyanide solution is captured and reused.

Mandated monitors are built into the pads to detect even the smallest leak, which is quickly fixed.

What happens to all of the overburden and discarded rock? Three storage areas will be used. One will be the mined out Globe Hill-Ironclad area where the material will be put into the Ironclad mine and the Globe Hill mine. Another overburden storage area is just south of the Cresson mine where the material will be used to help stabilize the historic Carlton Mill tailings. In the last stages of mining, the used material will go back into the surface pit created at one end of the Cresson mine area, while mining is going on at the other end.

Nineteen different state, county, city, and federal agencies have been involved in issuing permits and checking safety and the reconstruction of the mined areas. The company has posted a performance bond of more than $17 million with the state to insure that all reclamation and environmental requirements will be met.

During the construction of the plant and facilities in 1993, the company spent more than $19.3 million in Teller County and Colorado for payroll, goods, and services. Cripple Creek is the county seat of Teller County.

In 1994 over 300 contract workers were employed by the company for construction. Now that the facility is up and running in 1995, 254 workers are employed on a full-time and continuing basis. The annual payroll is over $4 million, by far the largest of any firm in Teller County. More than 75 percent of the firm's employees live in Teller County, most in Victor and Cripple Creek.

The county will also benefit from taxes the company pays. Property and production taxes will bring $2 million into the county treasury.

The company is active in preserving the rich history of the Cripple Creek Mining District. Several roadside exhibits and others inside the city of Victor will explain what has gone before in the mining areas and what's happening today. Also under way are exhibits to refurbish the large flat-rope hoist at the Gold Coin mine, put up an ore sorting machinery display, and set up a self-guided tour of the Independence Mill foundations. An overlook at the Cresson mine will let visitors view the current mining methods.

What is at stake in the huge outlay of development money that the CC&V Mining Company has made? Engineers have projected that in the tested areas, there are more than two million ounces of gold that can be recovered by the leaching process.

The price of gold fluctuates daily, but if it remains around $400 per ounce, that is a total gross income of $800 million for the company over the next eight to ten years.

That's a lot of cash in anybody's jeans. Say the Cripple Creek Bonanza was discovered today. How much would the gold taken out of there be worth at $400 an ounce? Somewhere around $1.09 billion. Not bad. Even so, Cripple Creek in the 1990s and into the 2000s will settle for the $800 million.

The Cripple Creek Burros

One small heritage of the Cripple Creek Bonanza days walks the street of the small town most days now. In fact there are eleven of them at this writing. They come and go, wander where they want to, get in the way of traffic, and sometimes get hit by cars.

They are the eleven pampered and loved Cripple Creek burros that inhabit this small town where their ancestors once toiled all day long deep in the hard rock mines.

Burros first came into Cripple Creek with the prospectors. No well-equipped prospector would be without one. Bob Womack never used one, but he only prospected close by to his cabin. Winfield Scott Stratton had several burros in his seventeen years of prospecting.

Today the Cripple Creek burros get special treatment. They are cared for by the Two Mile High Club in town. Members see that the animals are fed, watered, and generally taken care of. A Burro Master is named each year with the overall responsibility of feeding and caring for the burros.

The club took over the shepherding of the burros back in 1960 because the animals had increased to a herd of thirty and were getting in all sorts of trouble. The "Jacks," the males, would go on spells of fighting with each other by lashing out with their hind feet trying to hit the offending burro. Too often the hooves stove in the side of a resident's or a tourist's car, and there was makeup money to pay.

The club agreed to keep no more than fifteen burros in town and to get rid of most of the jacks to mellow down the herd.

Now and then one of the burros will dart out between cars or some other unseen spot and get hit by a car. Then emergency care is given.

Upkeep for the burros costs $300 a year, which is raised by the club each year during Donkey Derby Days. The burros are hauled over to Victor, six miles away, and riders draw lots for the animals. Then they must catch and "ride" that numbered burro back to Cripple Creek. Since the feisty little animals are not broken, this riding is often hilarious.

Back in Cripple Creek while the crowd waits for the riders to come, the outhouse race is held. Teams see who can pull their outhouse up Bennett Avenue the fastest and win.

In the early days, many burros were used to pack into the hard-to-get-to mines and claims. These were called Jack Trains, and they hauled in lots of freight. They were used more extensively in the San Juans than in Cripple Creek. No railroad served that mining community, and strings of twenty burros would wind up the hill, taking in much-needed supplies and equipment to the miners.

Some burros were used in the Cripple Creek mines in the early days. One source said that burros were pulling ore cars in the Cresson mine as late as 1938.

The burros were used in the mines to haul ore cars, but they weren't quite as sturdy or as strong as the work demanded.

Soon the miners began to use "ginetts." As near as can be determined, these animals were small mules but still larger and stronger than the burros so they could pull more. The usual procedure was to fill the ore cars at the tunnel face and then take off the brakes and let them roll in a controlled descent down the 3 percent grade to the shaft.

Where possible the Cripple Creek tunnels and drifts were dug out at a 3 percent upward grade. This meant that gravity would take over and roll the cars at no expense to the shaft. As the ore cars rolled forward, the ginett walked along behind them. At the shaft, the ore car would be rolled onto the cage or platform and hauled to the surface.

When empty, the ore cars were returned to the working level. Here was where the ginetts came into use. The ginett now was harnessed to a string of empty ore cars and pulled them back up the 3 percent grade to the head of the tunnel where the gold ore waited.

When electric engines came into use, they took the place of the ginetts and usually hauled the ore cars both ways.

For years the ginetts were used underground. There was a standard procedure that evolved for the animals. They had to be taken into the mine carefully. They were laid down and all four legs were folded up and tied against their belly. Then they were hoisted onboard a cage and dropped down to their work tunnel at the proper level. Below they were hoisted up, their legs untied, and they walked away unhurt.

When they weren't working, they were kept in a dug-out room in the mine. There they had hay, feed, and water. The stable area had a wooden floor put down over the dirt so the mules wouldn't get fungus on their feet and hooves. The ginetts did a good job and for the most part were well treated.

The usual practice was to keep them underground for six months at a time. Then they were taken to the shaft, their legs folded and tied, put on the cage with a hoist, and taken back to the surface.

When the ginetts first came out of the mine, they all wore sacks over their heads so the sun wouldn't be too bright on their eyes. After a few days the sacks were taken off. It's not clear how long the ginetts had on their fresh air time before they went back into the mines.

No reliable information is at hand, but we believe that the burros and the ginetts were not used for long in the mines when electrical power and small towing engines were available for use to do the hauling.

Still it's a bit of nostalgia to watch the roaming free burros work their way across Bennett Avenue and wander down toward the little stream called Cripple Creek searching for a spot of fresh grass to graze on.

Usually the burros are brought into town in May and allowed to roam during the tourist season. Then sometime in October the Two Mile High Club transports them back to their winter pasture so they'll be ready for another "showtime" next summer.

From time to time the herd must be cut down to keep it within limits. One such small burro became a birthday present for a nearby ranch woman, Celinda Kaelin, of the Twin Creek Ranch in Florissant. Now all grown up, Birdie is still smaller than the ranch horses.

Horses in a herd tend to pick on the smallest, so Birdie would have been the natural target. Instead of the horse pasture, Birdie was put in with the steers and one black Angus bull. Guess what happened? Here's the tale in the form of a poem by Mrs. Harold Kaelin.

BIRDIE AND THE BULL
by
Celinda Reynolds Kaelin

Dedicated to Rosie Cunningham, my dear friend.

The stately old pine tree gently
played with Brother Wind,
As he whistled and danced
in and through her spiny limbs.

Casting long shadows o'er the
tiny Burro's bed
As Brother Eagle glided circles
in clear blue sky above his head.

Little, lonely Burro—culled from the
herd at Cripple Creek
Coal black stripe across his withers,
pale dove gray upon his cheek.

Across the pasture then appeared
Alfalfa in all his might,
Muscles rippling down his back,
the Black Angus bull hove into sight.

He snorted and bellowed, then
started 'cross the blue sage
Birdie jumped, then answered, but
with talk of love, not rage.

Slowly trotting toward each other,
suspense now filled he air.
Bull and Burro met, nuzzled one the
other, and became an inseparable pair.

Taking a Chance

From the earliest days, gambling had been as much a
part of Cripple Creek as the gold mines themselves. The
miners found the gambling halls and the games in the saloons and dance halls to be a pleasant diversion after all day
pounding a drill a thousand feet underground.

After being outlawed for a long, long time, gambling
came back to Cripple Creek in October of 1991. It happened
this way. A statewide referendum was held to say yes or no
to Las Vegas-style gambling in three cities in Colorado.
Cripple Creek was one of them.

The move for gambling in Cripple Creek came mainly from the merchants and those who wanted to put gambling into their current hotels and cafes in the village. More and more the people of Cripple Creek realized their town was now mostly a tourist attraction, and they figured that the addition of gambling would draw a lot of tourist traffic.

Today, four years after gambling began in Cripple Creek, it is firmly established as a big factor in the economic health of the town. There were twenty-four casinos at last count, but they come and go and more new, larger ones are planned along historic Bennett Avenue.

The casinos can do what the Colorado referendum calls Limited Stakes Gambling. That means they can use Las Vegas-type slot machines with nickel to five-dollar bets. The casinos have from 50 to 400 slots and video poker machines.

The only other type of gambling allowed is poker and blackjack—no roulette wheel, no baccarat. Neither can players sit in on games played a hundred years ago in Cripple Creek such as faro, three-card monte, Boston, seven-up or euchre.

Some of the casinos are now talking about putting in bingo games. Bingo in Colorado is controlled not by the Colorado Gaming Commission which sets standards for the gambling, but by the Colorado Secretary of State.

Look for bingo and keeno to come to the town before long.

Cripple Creek has about 650 year-round residents. On good weather weekends the gamblers descend on the little village. They come by cars and by the busload from Colorado Springs, Pueblo, and Canon City. The bus rides are free, paid for by the casino owners. The patrons flood into the casino, bars, restaurants, hotels, and the dozens of gift shops and small stores that cater to the tourist and gambling crowd.

Victor, six miles from Cripple Creek and a sister in the gold mining of yesteryear, has about 300 people now, down from 12,000 during its bonanza mining days in the 1890s. Victor was one of the other towns that asked to have gambling when the referendum was taken. Later Victor officials decided they didn't want gambling there afterall. One resident of Victor who works in Cripple Creek said she was glad that they don't have gambling in her town.

More and larger gambling casinos are expected in Cripple Creek. Some of those already there were made by saving the face of the old buildings on Bennett Avenue, then gutting the rest of the buildings and putting up whole new structures designed to hold up the heavy gambling machines and the hoped-for hundreds of people.

You can play games of chance in Cripple Creek from 8:00 A.M. until 2:00 A.M. Sorry, there's no round-the-clock gambling yet at Cripple Creek the way it is in Las Vegas. But it could come to that down the line some time.

Now with gold mining back in modern day Cripple Creek, it somehow seems natural that the new boom in town should include gambling as well. What would all of the ghosts of those miners from the Cresson or the Independence or the El Paso say when they walk down Bennett Avenue after a tough day a couple of thousand feet below ground hammering out gold ore, when there's no place a man can have some fun gambling? Just wouldn't seem right to the ghosts of all of those high-living miners.

There's More

The Chamber of Commerce says there's more than mining and gambling in Cripple Creek. One thing that's hard to beat is the clear mountain air. That's air at 9,494 feet, so bring your oxygen bottle along. No, it isn't that bad, but the higher altitude means less oxygen in the ambient air, and it takes a little getting used to. You'll want to take more pauses and stops in your tour and drink more water.

Don't try your regular two-mile run the first day in town, you might not make it.

What else is in modern-day Cripple Creek? There is the longest running melodrama in the United States staged at the Imperial Hotel. You can visit a restored working gold mine, the Mollie Kathleen, a half mile out of town. There you can descend to 1,000 feet below the surface and see how gold used to be mined in Cripple Creek. As a bonus you'll get a free sample of real gold ore.

You can ride on the Cripple Creek and Victor narrow gauge railway. Visit the historic town of Victor only six miles away, take a ride on a horse-pulled buggy, and visit the Cripple Creek District Museum in the old railroad terminal building.

At the right time of the year you can enjoy cross-country skiing, golfing, hiking, and horseback riding. Remember, you long hitters, that your golf ball is going to go a lot farther when it starts at nearly two miles in the air.

That's about it. A booming, raucous, hard-driving mining town of 25,000 people at the turn of the century, it is now a rather laid-back, slowed down, gentler home to 650 people who are willing to share it with you.

"YEP, GREAT, GREAT, GREAT GRANDPA USED TO WORK IN THE MINES but I don't have to. I play around town all day, get fed and taken care of. I can wander all over Cripple Creek, and I'm supposed to have the right of way on the streets. Some tourists don't know that. Be careful! Come and see me sometime." A. Burro. (Photo Courtesy Cripple Creek District Museum)

Bibliography

Cakkey, Morris, *Rails Around Gold Hill*, World Press, Denver, CO., 1955.

Canfield, John G., *Mines And Mining Men of Colorado*, Canfield Publishers, Denver, CO., 1893.

Cripple Creek And Victor Gold Mining Company, *Summary of Amendment 6 to Permit M-80-244, The Cresson Project*, Company papers, Cripple Creek CO., 1994.

Cripple Creek And Victor Gold Mining Company, booklet of advertisements run in Teller County newspapers, 1992.

Cripple Creek Chamber of Commerce, *Cripple Creek Centennial Program*, Chamber of Commerce, 1992.

Cripple Creek Prospector, Newspaper, December 29, 1892.

Cripple Creek Crusher, Newspaper, February 24, 1893.

Drake, Raymond L., *The Last Gold Rush*, Pollux Press, Victor, CO., 1983.

Feitz, Leland, *A Pictorial History of Cripple Creek*, Little London Press, Colorado Springs, CO., 1990.

Feitz, Leland, *Cripple Creek Railroads*, Little London Press, Colorado Springs, CO., 1968.

Feitz, Leland, *Cripple Creek, The World's Greatest Gold Camp*, Little London Press, Colorado Springs, CO., 1967.

Feitz, Leland, *Ghost Towns of Cripple Creek District*, Little London Press, Colorado Springs, CO., 1974.

Feitz, Leland, *Victor, Colorado's City of Mines*, Little London Press, Colorado Springs, CO., 1974.

Feitz, Leland, *Myers Avenue, Cripple Creek's Red Light District*, Little London Press, Colorado Springs, CO., 1967.

Great Divide Printing Co., *Divide Dispatch*, Volume IV, No. 2., Divide, CO., 1994.

Bibliography

Griffith, William H., *The History of Cripple Creek, Cripple Creek Times*, Cripple Creek, CO., 1903.

Hills, Fred, *Official Manual of the Cripple Creek District*, Fred Hills, Colorado Springs, CO., 1900.

Horsley, Albert E., *The Confessions and Autobiography of Harry Orchard*, McClure CO., 1907.

Ives, James R., *City Directory Cripple Creek of 1891 and 1893*, Gazetter Publishing Co., Denver, CO., 1891, 1893.

Journal of the West, Cripple Creek Law & Order (chapter *Journal Of The West*, 1963.

Kimmett, Leo, *Florissant, Colorado*, (Revised Edition) Master Printers, Canon City, CO., 1986.

Lee, Mabel, *Cripple Creek Days*, Doubleday & Co., New York, NY., 1958.

Mazzulla, Fred and Jo, *Pikes Peak Gold*, Barbarossa Press, Victor, CO., 1956.

Rastall, Benjamin McKie, *Labor History of the Cripple Creek District*, University of Wisconsin Press, 1908.

Rickard, T.A., *A History of American Mining*, McGraw-Hill, 1933.

Sargent & Rohrabacher, *The Fortunes Of A Decade*, The *Evening Telegraph*, Colorado Springs, CO., 1900.

Sprague, Marshall, *Money Mountain*, Little Brown and Company, Boston, MA., 1953.

U.S. Bureau of Mines, *Mineral Yearbooks Area Reports*, Washington, D.C., 1950 through 1975.

U.S. Geological Survey, *Professional Paper No. 54 PL XXIX*, U.S. Government, Washington, D.C., 1905.

Victor Daily Record, Various early editions, Victor, CO.

Waters, Frank, *Midas of the Rockies*, Denver University Press, 1949.

Wolle, Muriel S., *Stampede To Timberline*, Muriel Wolle, Boulder, CO., 1949.

218

Other Books From Republic of Texas Press

100 Days in Texas: The Alamo Letters
by Wallace O. Chariton

Alamo Movies
by Frank Thompson

At Least 1836 Things You Ought to Know About Texas but Probably Don't
by Doris L. Miller

Classic Clint: The Laughs and Times of Clint Murchison, Jr.
by Dick Hitt

Defense of a Legend: Crockett and the de la Peña Diary
by Bill Groneman

Don't Throw Feathers at Chickens: A Collection of Texas Political Humor
by Charles Herring, Jr. and Walter Richter

Eight Bright Candles: Courageous Women of Mexico
by Doris E. Perlin

Exploring the Alamo Legends
by Wallace O. Chariton

From an Outhouse to the White House
by Wallace O. Chariton

The Funny Side of Texas
by Ellis Posey and John Johnson

Ghosts Along the Texas Coast
by Docia Schultz Williams

The Great Texas Airship Mystery
by Wallace O. Chariton

Great Texas Golf: A Complete Directory to All Texas Golf Courses
by Pat Seelig

How the Cimarron River Got Its Name and Other Stories About Coffee
by Ernestine Sewell Linck

The Last Great Days of Radio
by Lynn Woolley

Noble Brutes: Camels on the American Frontier
by Eva Jolene Boyd

Outlaws in Petticoats and Other Notorious Texas Women
by Gail Drago and Ann Ruff

Rainy Days in Texas Funbook
by Wallace O. Chariton

Slitherin' 'Round Texas
by Jim Dunlap

Spirits of San Antonio and South Texas
by Docia Schultz Williams and Reneta Byrne

Texas Highway Humor
by Wallace O. Chariton

Texas Politics in My Rearview Mirror
by Waggoner Carr and Byron Varner

Texas Tales Your Teacher Never Told You
by Charles F. Eckhardt

Texas Wit and Wisdom
by Wallace O. Chariton

That Cat Won't Flush
by Wallace O. Chariton

That Old Overland Stagecoaching
by Eva Jolene Boyd

This Dog'll Hunt
by Wallace O. Chariton

Call Wordware Publishing, Inc. for names of the bookstores in your area: (214) 423-0090

To The Tyrants Never Yield: A
Texas Civil War Sampler
by Kevin R. Young
Tragedy at Taos: The Revolt
of 1847
by James A. Crutchfield
A Trail Rider's Guide to Texas
by Mary Elizabeth Sue Goldman

Unsolved Texas Mysteries
by Wallace O. Chariton
Western Horse Tales
Edited by Don Worcester
Wild Camp Tales
by Mike Blakely

Seaside Press

The Bible for Busy People
Book 1: The Old Testament
by Mark Berrier Sr.

Critter Chronicles
by Jim Dunlap

Dallas Uncovered
by Larenda Lyles Roberts

Dirty Dining: A Cookbook,
and More, for Lovers
by Ginnie Siena Bivona

Exotic Pets: A Veterinary
Guide for Owners
by Shawn Messonnier, D.V.M.

I Never Wanted to Set the
World on Fire, but Now That
I'm 50, Maybe Its a Good Idea
by Bob Basso, Ph.D.

Just Passing Through
by Beth Beggs

Kingmakers
by John R. Knaggs

Lives and Works of the
Apostles
by Russell A. Stultz

Los Angeles Uncovered
by Frank Thompson

Only: The Last Dinosaur
by Jim Dunlap

Seattle Uncovered
by JoAnn Roe

San Antonio Uncovered
by Mark Louis Rybczyk

A Sure Reward
by B.J. Smagula

Survival Kit for Today's
Family
by Bill Swetmon

They Don't Have to Die
by Jim Dunlap

Twin Cities Uncovered
by The Arthurs

Your Puppy's First Year
by Shawn Messonnier, D.V.M.

Call Wordware Publishing, Inc. for names of the
bookstores in your area: (214) 423-0090